Too Perfect

Too Perfect

When Being in Control Gets Out of Control

Allan E. Mallinger, M.D., and Jeannette De Wyze

CLARKSON POTTER/PUBLISHERS

NEW YORK

Grateful acknowledgment is made to the following for permission to reprint previously published material:

Alfred A. Knopf, Inc.: an excerpt from *The Accidental Tourist* by Anne Tyler. Copyright © 1985 by Anne Tyler Moldarressi.

Bantam Books: an excerpt from *Journey of Awakening* by Ram Dass.

Crown Publishers, Inc.: an excerpt from "Taking the Manly Way Out" from *Dave Barry Talks Back* by Dave Barry. Copyright © 1991 by Dave Barry.

E P Dutton: an excerpt from *The Boy Who Couldn't Stop Washing* by Judith L. Rapoport.

HarperCollins Publishers: an excerpt from *The Addictive Organization* by Anne W. Schaef and Dianne Fassel; an excerpt from *You Can't Go Home Again* by Thomas Wolfe.

Published by Clarkson N. Potter, Inc.,
201 East 50th Street, New York, New York 10022.
Member of the Crown Publishing Group.
CLARKSON POTTER, POTTER and colophon
are trademarks of Clarkson N. Potter, Inc.

Manufactured in the United States of America

Library of Congress Cataloging-in-Publication Data
Mallinger, Allan E.
Too perfect: when being in control gets out of control
/Allan Mallinger and Jeannette De Wyze.
1. Perfectionism (Personality trait); obsessiveness
2. Psychology, Pathological.
I. De Wyze, Jeannette. II. Title.
RC569.5.P45M35 1991 91-8662
158'.1—dc20   91-8662
ISBN 0-517-57565-5

10 9 8 7 6 5 4 3

For Murphy, Jesse, Noah, and Ben

A.E.M.

For Steve, Michael, Elliott,
and The Cosmic Scorekeeper,
wherever he/she lurks

J.D.

ACKNOWLEDGMENTS

The ideas in this book are a distillate of my own observations and the writings and teachings of many others.

All therapists are deeply indebted to Freud for his now classic descriptions of both the obsessive personality and the obsessive compulsive disorder, as well as literally dozens of seminal and revolutionary concepts that are now automatic components of every psychiatrist's training.

Recent theorists such as Harry Stack Sullivan, David Shapiro, and Leon Salzman greatly enriched our understanding of the obsessive personality style. Sullivan described how obsessiveness is a logical result of an anxious child's attempt to gain a sense of security within the family. Shapiro pioneered the theory that obsessiveness is much more than a set of defenses and adaptions; it's a style of *being*—of thinking, of speaking, of handling feelings and relationships.

Salzman advanced our understanding still further. He delineated the core dynamic central to the obsessive style: namely, the illusory attempt to deal with anxiety engendered by the perception of one's own vulnerability in a universe filled with risks.

I am also indebted to the cognitive theorists—Beck, Bieber, Ellis— for clarifying the central role of irrational beliefs and assumptions that underlie and perpetuate dysfunctional behavior, and for offering us therapeutic tools to deal with these distortions.

I particularly want to acknowledge the late Irving Bieber, M.D., beloved mentor and friend, for his patient guidance and support, and his vigorous encouragement to write, even when I was a rebellious psychiatric resident. I only hope that I am passing on to my own residents, patients, and readers some small reflection of his wisdom and humanity.

I am also grateful to friends and colleagues who took the time to read and critique drafts of the manuscript, especially: Victoria Brown, Maureen Gevirtz, Paula Kriner, Paul Krueger, Nan Van Gelder, and Stephen Wolfe.

The following people made helpful comments and suggestions: Paul Koprowski, Judith Liu, Ellen Margolis, Kathleen Murphy Mallinger, Irving Osowsky, and Sandra Sveine.

—*Allan E. Mallinger, M.D.*

CONTENTS

AUTHOR'S NOTE

Throughout the book, I use many case studies to illustrate various aspects of obsessiveness (disguised, of course, to protect my patients' identities). Often the person described is actually a composite of several patients with similar psychological characteristics.

Many of these clinical vignettes include exchanges drawn verbatim from tapes or from notes I took during sessions. Some have been edited for clarification. But most of the quotes represent exactly what was said, given the limitations of note-taking.

Introduction

In my nineteen years of practice, I have always found my obsessive patients to be among the most intriguing. And early on, it became clear to me that many laypeople also wanted to know more about obsessiveness. When I lectured about personality styles before adult-education classes, most of the questions I was asked seemed to be about the obsessive personality. Soon I began receiving invitations to talk about that topic alone, and there were seldom empty seats; in fact, overflow audiences stood at the back of the hall. Often my listeners would respond in ways that suggested they were all too familiar with the various obsessive traits I was describing.

Before professional audiences, too, I detected an avid interest in the subject. In after-class discussions with psychiatric residents and other mental-health professionals, I learned that many of these therapists were finding their obsessive patients particularly challenging and, in some cases, downright frustrating to work with. Obsessive people often are controlling or cerebral or distrustful or secretive or emotionally constricted or resistant to change or all of the above, any one of which can make therapy difficult. I found my colleagues to be hungry for any ideas that might help them.

This prompted my decision to expand my lecture notes into a monograph for therapists, discussing the basic dynamics of the obsessive personality and pointing out potential pitfalls in working with obsessive patients. When I showed a summary of my proposed monograph to friends, several claimed that they recognized their *own* personalities in my accounts, and said they had experienced, or were currently having, many of the same difficulties as the patients I described. Their comments inspired me to change the focus of my project, and to write directly to the obsessive person and to people in relationships with obsessives.

That decision presented me with a particular challenge in regard to giving advice. When I practice face-to-face therapy with my patients, I become very familiar with their psychological makeup. The intimate connections between us guide me in what I say and what I avoid saying; what will help and what may do more harm than good. And when I do say something, I receive continual feedback, both verbal and nonverbal, as to how my patient is reacting. My "reading" of this feedback enables me to decide what to say or do next, or whether to be silent. When my "patient" is a reader, however, I have none of this information.

I also believe that specific advice as the avenue to change is overrated. Even in face-to-face therapy, when I've done very brief, direct, concrete interventions (e.g., "Go home and do these three things"), and have later asked much-improved patients what aspect of our work helped the most, they often say such things as "I felt that you cared about me"; "You seemed optimistic that I would get better"; "You didn't seem to be judging me"; "When I understood what was causing my behavior, I was able to change it." Only when I ask specifically, "But what about the techniques that I taught you and the homework you did?" do they respond, "Oh, yes. That helped too."

The point is that even when therapists give very specific instructions for handling psychological problems, if the patient improves, we may too quickly jump to faulty conclusions about what "worked." Though suggestions are often helpful, many people are helped at least as much by the therapeutic relationship itself and by gaining insight into their problems and self-defeating behaviors.

For this reason, I believe that my readers' most important tool will be *understanding*—coming to a clearer and deeper awareness of obsessive traits and of how they may be causing problems in everyday life, coupled with some idea of how things could be better if certain changes were made. I will offer specific suggestions only when I feel they are likely to be helpful.

Unfortunately, obsessives, perhaps more than any other group of patients, have a need to believe that there is a specific and clear answer to every question; an unambiguous, conflict-free solution to every problem. In therapy, obsessive patients often believe at some level that *I* have the answers, and that if only they give me enough accurate information I'll eventually be able to produce a sort of prescription for happiness, detailing exactly what needs to be done—something they might follow as one would a road map. Usually they are disappointed to learn the truth: that the pathway to positive change is anything but clear, especially in the beginning.

It's true that as a therapist I can help in many ways: through the use of specific behavioral, cognitive, and psychodynamic techniques; through the enhancement of insight; and, probably most important, through the amazing power of this strange, loving bond we call the therapeutic relationship. But the therapeutic "hour" is usually only forty-five minutes a week. It's an island of time for honest communication, reflection, clarification, and encouragement, a starting point. In the end, each person must use his or her own new insights, creativity, courage, and motivation as a springboard for his or her own trial solutions. In the same way, I hope readers will use this book as a starting point to positive change.

ONE

The Obsessive Personality

When we would pursue virtues to their extremes on either side,
vices present themselves. . . . We find fault with perfection itself.

—PASCAL,
Pensées

This is a book about people who are too perfect for their own good.

You know them. You may be one of them. And if you are, you have much to be proud of. You're one of the solid, good people of the world: honest, reliable, hardworking, responsible, exacting, self-controlled.

But for many people there is also a dark side to this perfection. The very traits that bring them success, respect, and trust can also cause them serious problems. These people aren't fully able to savor relationships with others and with the world at large, nor are they at ease with themselves in their universe. Consider:

- The person so driven to meet professional and personal goals that she can't abandon herself to a few hours of undirected leisure without feeling guilty or undisciplined.

- The person so preoccupied with *making the right choice* that he has difficulty making even relatively simple decisions usually regarded as pleasurable: buying a new stereo; choosing where to go on vacation.
- The person so finicky that his pleasure is spoiled if everything isn't "just so."
- The "thinkaholic" whose keen, hyperactive mind all too often bogs her down in painful worry and rumination.
- The perfectionist, whose need to improve and polish every piece of work chronically causes her to devote much more time than necessary to even inconsequential assignments.
- The person so intent upon finding the ultimate romantic mate that he seems unable to commit to *any* long-term relationship.
- The person so acclimated to working long hours that she can't bring herself to cut back, even when confronted with evidence that the overwork is ruining her health or her family relationships.
- The procrastinator who feels angry at his "laziness"—unaware that the real reason he is unable to undertake tasks is that his need to do them flawlessly makes them loom impossibly large.

These are just a few of the behaviors common to people who have the personality type that psychiatrists call *obsessive.* This term and the related term, *compulsive,* have crept into our everyday language to a striking degree. This person is "obsessed" with baseball. That one is a "compulsive" shopper. Recent articles and books have also made the lay public aware of obsessive-compulsive disorder (OCD), the malady that drives its sufferers to such acts as repeated hand-washing, checking routines, or other paralyzing rituals.

When I use the term *obsessive,* however, I mean something quite different. I'm referring to a *personality type,* not to an isolated behavior or clinical disorder like OCD.

If there is a single quality that characterizes obsessive people it is a powerful, unconscious need to feel in control—of themselves, of others, and of life's risks. One of the primary ways in which this need manifests itself is perfectionism. A whole family of personality traits is rooted in these two needs—to be in control and to be "perfect." These include:

- a fear of making errors
- a fear of making a wrong decision or choice
- a strong devotion to work
- a need for order or firmly established routine
- frugality
- a need to know and follow the rules
- emotional guardedness
- a tendency to be stubborn or oppositional
- a heightened sensitivity to being pressured or controlled by others
- an inclination to worry, ruminate, or doubt
- a need to be above criticism—moral, professional, or personal
- cautiousness
- a chronic inner pressure to use every minute productively

By my definition, someone is obsessive if his or her personality is predominantly colored by traits from this family—in any combination. Many of these traits, when they aren't exaggerated or rigid, are valuable qualities. It's hard to imagine someone succeeding in our society today without some degree of self-discipline, for example, or some desire to work hard and avoid errors. But some people are "too perfect." The obsessive traits in their personality are so dominant and inflexible that these virtues actually *cause* a host of problems.

In my practice I see new examples of such self-generated anguish every day. And at the same time I see how *unaware* most obsessives are that they're harming themselves; they recoil from any hint that their heavy burdens could be self-imposed. Most have grown up believing that you can *never* be too careful, hardworking, thorough, prepared, or organized. In fact, they're often proudest of the very traits that cause them the most harm.

Rarely do my obsessive patients come to me because they feel there's anything wrong with their attitudes or lifestyles. Instead they come seeking help with some specific symptom or external stressor. Maybe they've begun suffering from baffling anxiety or gastrointestinal ailments. Or they may be having trouble coping with some distressing life event: a serious career reversal or a work block that threatens their urgent need to achieve. Often a spouse or lover has insisted that they get some help.

In Laura's case, it was her internist's suggestion that led her to me. For months this patient had felt drained of any joy or zest for life, and her sleep and appetite both were suffering. Laura initially felt baffled by her inability to simply shake off her feelings of sadness. But she was a bright, sensitive, insightful person, and was quickly able to isolate several factors that were feeding her melancholy.

Much of Laura's self-esteem was inextricably intertwined with her image of herself as an achiever who invariably dazzled people with her accomplishments. The exemplary child of prominent professionals, she had graduated with top honors from a prestigious Eastern university, then had embarked on a business career in which she swiftly rose to become the marketing director for a highly successful new clothing retailer. Almost immediately, people within her company came to think of Laura as someone who could handle any problem or shoulder any task, no matter how difficult.

Her private life, however, was another matter. She was unhappy with her marriage and had been thinking about getting a divorce, but she felt terribly frustrated by her inability to make a final decision. She also felt totally burned out by her job. Because she had trouble delegating tasks and felt she had to be all things to all people, she really did have a crushing work load, which was made even more onerous by the incredibly high standards by which she judged her own work. Once Laura told me that she felt truly relaxed only when she was in a darkened movie theater. Even at home, she was constantly either working or feeling guilty about ignoring one chore or another.

Clearly, Laura had reasons to feel troubled, but she didn't realize that she could behave any differently. It took time and effort for her to see how much *she* was contributing to her own misery. As I got to know her, I learned that Laura's father had been a picky, judgmental man with inflexible views on the "right" way to do everything. Laura thus grew up believing that in order to earn her father's love (an almost impossible task, since he was so hard to please), she had to perform flawlessly. As an adult, Laura's continuing abhorrence of making mistakes was preventing her from taking action in her marriage, and was vastly complicating her work life. At the same time, her unremitting self-criticism soured her ability to truly enjoy any of her own substantial achievements.

Raymond, a surgeon in a university hospital, came to see me only at the insistence of his wife, Abbe, a corporate architect. Married for fifteen years, both were workaholics who had grown used to spending most of their time apart. When I met the two of them, Abbe had encountered a career crisis and needed support from her husband— support that she felt was totally absent. Abbe also charged that her domineering husband constantly "bullied" her—passing judgment on everything from her cooking to her political opinions. As a result she had come to feel chronically inhibited and constrained in her own home. Even more disturbing to her was the extent to which Raymond failed to share his feelings with her. Not only did she feel no sense of intimacy with him, she felt unloved and terribly lonely.

It was true, Raymond acknowledged, that he had trouble trusting people, even people he loved. He justified this distrustfulness by recalling the various individuals who had let him down over the years. Raymond's childhood offered further clues into his guardedness. His father had been a stern and critical man who never seemed appreciative of any of his son's many achievements. To protect himself from crushing feelings of rejection, Raymond had, early on, developed a thick shell. But Raymond insisted that he *did* care about his wife and she should know it; her needs for more overt displays of affection from him were just indications of her own insecurity. For every one of her specific criticisms he had a forceful, eloquent defense.

After just three sessions, Raymond canceled our meetings, saying he would reschedule another appointment soon. I didn't hear from him again, however, until several months later. It was hard to reconcile the anguished voice on the phone with the aloof, intimidating figure I had met before. When he arrived at the office, Raymond told me that he had lost twenty pounds and admitted he was seriously contemplating suicide. Abbe had openly embarked upon an affair with another man and Raymond was absolutely devastated at the prospect of losing her. Nothing else in his life was as important as she was, he told me, weeping. If he *had* to change, somehow, in order to win her back, then he would try to change. But I could see that Raymond still didn't fully understand that his own perfectionism, guardedness, and need for control had helped set him up for this personal tragedy. We met for several sessions and he did appear to make some progress, but then he once again abruptly dropped out of therapy.

The Causes of Obsessiveness

Both Laura and Raymond happened to have in common a parent whose love seemed conditional, tied to such things as how well they performed, and how "good" or capable they were. Because they also perceived their parents as critical, negativistic, and hard to please, these bright, sensitive children felt caught in a no-win situation, never feeling that they were good enough—never feeling secure. Similar stories about childhood experiences are common in my practice.

Let me stress that patients in therapy are reporting *their* perceptions of their early childhood experiences. It may well be that the person who will become strongly obsessive perceives his world and its expectations of him differently from other children.

Many of my patients also perceived a parent's words and actions as contradictory. While their words may have conveyed love and concern, the parent's behaviors and apparent attitudes reflected self-interest and often a lack of empathy for the child. "Whenever my parents wouldn't let me do something, they always made it sound rational," one patient told me. "I remember having to take piano lessons, which I hated. My parents made it sound as if it was for my own good, but it wasn't. They both had wanted to study music but had been unable to do so." Another patient put it this way: "My parents insisted on being in control, and it took all the starch out of me. Over time, my spirit was eroded, broken."

Many patients have reiterated this experience: conformance to family and social rules having more importance to the parents than whatever the child was thinking, feeling, wanting, or fearing. A significant number of my obsessive patients reveal that they didn't feel *liked* by one or both parents. These patients felt they'd been "good" children and had made real efforts to meet their parents' expectations, only to find a lack of consistent appreciation, or worse, criticism.

I believe that—to some extent—perfectionism, caution, drivenness, and other obsessive traits are indeed adaptations. They not only quell some of the anxiety engendered by early feelings of insecurity, but also garner many obvious payoffs. Still, it is overly simplistic to conclude that early childhood experiences *alone* cause people to develop obsessive personalities. Humans are infinitely complex, and while family and subcultural values are hammer and anvil, to a point, the person's genetic and constitutional makeup is the "ore."

Scores of parents have told me of children who seemed picky, perfectionistic, contemplative, and cautious, almost from birth. "I remember making Christmas cookies with Max when he was barely two years old," one woman told me. "When a little piece of dough remained wedged in a corner of the cookie cutter, he insisted I throw the offending cookie away. I told him that the cookie was just fine, but he burst into tears and wailed that it wasn't perfect, so he wouldn't eat it. It was crazy! Later, in nursery school, he refused to fingerpaint with the other children; he thought it was too messy."

It wouldn't surprise me if scientists one day discovered specific biological underpinnings favoring the development of any of several personality styles, including the obsessive. Certainly the trend in psychiatry in the last several years has been to discover that more and more psychological and psychiatric problems such as schizophrenia and mood disorders in fact have strong biological roots.

In sum, the likeliest hypothesis as to the cause of obsessiveness is that some people have a constitutional predisposition for being obsessive, and it can be enhanced or minimized by early-life perceptions and experiences.

The Core of Obsessiveness: The Need for Control

Regardless of the psychobiological *causes* of obsessiveness, the *central dynamic* in the obsessive personality is that of control. Most of us, obsessives included, would allow that life is fundamentally unpredictable. As hard as the best-intentioned, most conscientious person might try, it is impossible to control every aspect of one's existence; we are vulnerable. Despite such lip service to these truths, however, *somewhere near the center of their inner being, far from their conscious awareness, obsessives are trying to deny this reality. Their subtle but constant efforts to control everything in the world around them (and inside them) are an attempt to do the impossible: to guarantee security; to assure safe passage through the risks and uncertainties of living.*

Sometimes these efforts may "work" for years. Their conscientiousness and thoroughness bring obsessives admiration in their workplace. They follow the laws and rules assiduously, so they rarely incur the disapproval of those in authority. They seldom are rejected in romantic encounters since they avoid situations that make them vulnerable, or they take preemptive action when they sense an affair is going awry, so that *they* may be the one to end it. They conform to the standards of their social groups, so they usually aren't ridiculed or ostracized. And the rewards for being responsible, consistent, alert to details, safety-conscious, and well organized are legion.

But all this security comes at a price. Though they may be inured to it, many strongly obsessive people are *suffering.* They may be unable to show their feelings or to trust anyone (even their closest loved ones) completely, and as a result live with the chilling sense of being fundamentally alone.

Many obsessives suffer the endless agony of having to do everything well—an unnecessary imperative that can ruin even the most enjoyable

9

of activities. Their fear of embarrassment and appearing less than perfect may keep them from trying new things.

They struggle daily under the weight of a massive inner rulebook, an overgrown sense of duty, responsibility, and fairness. Most obsessives rarely taste the joys of the moment; the present hardly exists for them. Even in their time off, many can't fully relax, or just play. Indeed, they never are really "off." Worries bedevil them as they plow through life doing the "right" things, hoping that caution, diligence, and sacrifice will pay off—someday.

Sometimes they're sadly disappointed. I think of the words of an eighty-five-year-old Kentucky woman named Nadine Stair. She wrote,

IF I HAD MY LIFE TO LIVE OVER

I'd like to make more mistakes next time. I'd relax. I would limber up. I would be sillier than I've been this trip. I would take fewer things seriously. I would take more chances. I would climb more mountains and swim more rivers. I would eat more ice cream and less beans. I would perhaps have more actual troubles, but I'd have fewer imaginary ones. You see, I'm one of those people who live sensibly and sanely hour after hour, day after day. Oh, I've had my moments, and if I had to do it over again, I'd have more of them. In fact, I'd try to have nothing else. Just moments, one after another, instead of living so many years ahead of each day. I've been one of those persons who never goes anywhere without a thermometer, a hot water bottle, a raincoat, and a parachute. If I had to do it again, I would travel lighter than I have.

No one can relive the part of his or her life that's already past. But if you are obsessive, and in pain, you *can* change your future to one with more personal pleasure and fulfillment.

A Self Test

The first step is recognizing and understanding the cluster of traits that constitute the obsessive personality. To help you determine if you (or a loved one) are obsessive, I've prepared the following questionnaire, intended as a further clarification of the family of obsessive traits.

1. Do you get caught up in details, whether you're preparing a report for work or cleaning out the garage at home? Yes

2. Is it hard for you to let go of a work project until it's just right—even if it takes much longer than it should? yes

3. Have you often been called picky or critical? Or do you feel you are? Yes

4. Is it important to you that your child, spouse, or subordinates at work perform certain tasks in a certain specific manner? yes

5. Do you have trouble making decisions? (For example, do you go back and forth before making a purchase, planning a vacation, or choosing what to order from a menu?) yes

6. After you do make a decision, do you find yourself second-guessing or doubting your choice? yes

7. Do you find it embarrassing to "lose control" and be emotional (e.g., to look nervous, weep, or raise your voice in anger)? yes

8. At the same time, do you sometimes find yourself wishing it were easier for you to show your feelings? yes

9. Do you have a particularly strong conscience, or do you often feel guilty? yes

10. Is self-discipline important to you? yes

11. Are you especially wary of being controlled, manipulated, overpowered, or "steam-rollered" by others? _yes_

12. Is it important for you to get a "good deal" in your financial transactions, or are you often suspicious of being "taken"? _yes_

13. Do you think you're more guarded than most people about sharing your possessions, time, or money? _yes_

14. Do you tend to be secretive? That is, are you reluctant to reveal your motives or feelings? _yes_

15. Is it hard for you to let yourself be dependent on others, rather than self-reliant? (For instance, are you uneasy about delegating tasks at work or hiring help with taxes or home repairs?) _yes_

16. Do you have trouble putting a problem out of your mind until it's resolved, even when you're doing other things? _yes_

17. In thinking about some future event, such as a vacation, a dinner party, or a job report, do you dwell upon the things that might go wrong? _yes_

18. Do you worry more than most people? _yes_

19. Do you derive a great deal of your sense of worth from being able to perform your job flawlessly? _yes_

20. Do you get extremely upset when someone is unhappy with or critical of a piece of work you have done, even when the criticism is mild or valid? _yes_

21. Do you feel that your family life, social life, or leisure-time enjoyment is being damaged or compromised by the amount of worry, time, or energy you put into work? _yes_

22. Do you feel guilty when you aren't getting something done, even in your time off (no matter how hard you've worked all week)? yes

23. Do you make lists of things you "should" do, even in your spare time? yes

24. Do even occasional "white lies" bother you? yes

25. Do you find it hard to trust that things will probably turn out for the best? yes

Interpreting Your Responses

If you find yourself answering "yes" to more than just a few of these questions, you (or your loved one) are probably at least somewhat obsessive. Now look once again at the questions to which you answered "yes," and for each one, answer a second question: Does this characteristic cause difficulties in relationships, work, or leisure activities, or does it interfere with your ability to enjoy life in general? If you answer "yes" to this *even once,* you will benefit from learning more about obsessiveness and about the possibility for change.

Before beginning, however, I offer this cautionary note: If you are strongly obsessive, you're a careful person who finds security in sameness and predictability. You're more wary of change and newness than the average person—and changing isn't easy for anyone!

But change is always possible. It may involve time and struggle. It may occasionally be painful. But it can be a journey toward a happier, more relaxed and fulfilling life.

The Myth of Control

*If Garp could have been granted one vast and naive wish, it would
have been that he could make the world safe. For children and
for grownups, the world struck Garp as unnecessarily perilous
for both.*

—JOHN IRVING,
The World According to Garp

E veryone needs some self-control, and some mastery over his or
her environment, just to survive. But many obsessives have a
disproportionate need for control—one that is driven and rigid,
rather than reasonable and flexible.

This exaggerated need stems from an irrational conviction that
perfect control can ensure safe passage through life. In my opinion,
every obsessive person subscribes to the myth that ultimate control is
possible, though in almost every case he or she is unaware of it. Like
some deeply buried tree root, the "Myth of Control" anchors and
constantly nourishes the controlled and controlling behavior so familiar to anyone close to the strongly obsessive person.

What are the roots of this myth? I believe that children who will
become obsessive are terrified by the awareness of their own vulnerability in a world they perceive as threatening and unpredictable. In order

to maintain a sense of calm and to navigate sanely through life, they must somehow ward off or deny this awareness. So they come to believe that, through control of themselves and their personal universe, they can protect themselves against the dangers in life, both real and imagined. If they could articulate the myth that motivates their behavior, they might say: "If I try hard enough, I can stay in control of *myself,* of *others,* and of all the *impersonal dangers* of life (injury, illness, death, etc.). In this way I can be certain of safe passage."

Obsessive people continue to embrace this myth at an unconscious level throughout their lives. Though they will acknowledge that such total control is impossible, the myth nonetheless continues to influence their behavior from its place deep within. In fact, to maintain their sense of well-being, many obsessives need frequent evidence reconfirming the myth in every sphere of life: self-control, control of others, and "global" control of impersonal factors.

Self-Control

Self-discipline is the mark of maturity, is it not? We all admire the person who eats and drinks in moderation; who works at maintaining a fit, well-conditioned body; who is even-tempered; who manages to persevere even at difficult, unsupervised tasks. But in their unconscious quest for absolute self-control, many obsessives carry such solid virtues to self-destructive extremes.

As I think back to my own days in medical school, I remember students who would not only study long hours but would deny themselves even the most legitimate breaks for eating, exercising, talking with other students, or entertainment. Would reasonable breaks really have caused a dip in their grade-point averages? Wouldn't an occasional Saturday off have improved the quality of their lives and their personal growth? The answers are obvious, but there was no way you could have convinced these people. They were deft at rationalizing their behavior (e.g., "I'm no genius—I need more study time.").

I call these reasons rationalizations because, while they may have been true, there was another, deeper and more powerful force driving these students to such extremes. Though they probably weren't conscious of it, many feared that if they let their self-control slip just once, they might have less of it the next time, and still less thereafter. They feared they would ultimately lose their hard-won diligence completely and become paralyzed or helpless, unable to accomplish anything. Of course this "thinking" goes on somewhere beneath the surface, where it doesn't have the benefit of scrutiny, analysis, and revision.

When obsessives lapse while dieting or trying to quit smoking or drinking, they may have trouble moving beyond their lapse and refocusing on the goal. Instead they're apt to feel distraught over the transgression, and to dwell on it. And why? Not because they seriously think one slip will make them fat, sick, or drunk, but rather because they lost control. They failed to make themselves do what they decided to do, and if such a slip occurred once, who knows where it could lead?

THINKING IN EXTREMES

These examples point up an important characteristic of many obsessives: their tendency to think in extremes. To yield to another person, for example, may be felt as a humiliating total capitulation. Similarly, to tell one lie, break one appointment, tolerate a spouse's criticism just once, or shed a single tear is to set a frightening precedent. One patient told me she hated to miss even a single workout because it made her feel she couldn't trust herself, and that frightened her.

This all-or-nothing thinking occurs partly because obsessives rarely live in the present. They think in terms of trends stretching into the future. *No* action is an isolated event; each is merely a part of something bigger, so every false step has major ramifications.

Such distorted thinking can cause a host of problems. I've known obsessives, for instance, who had trouble relaxing and enjoying first dates because they were so preoccupied with the possible remote consequences of such occasions. ("Would I want to marry this person?") In all-or-nothing thinking, one's perspective is badly distorted; there's a failure to step back and remind oneself that going out with someone *doesn't* commit one to any long-term romance.

Another consequence of such thinking is that it aggravates the pain of worry and rumination. Obsessives tend to envision the worst possible outcome of a scenario and then worry as if such a scenario had in fact come to pass. Or they will mentally magnify small personal gaffes into something far more serious. Some of my patients have had trouble sleeping after briefly losing their composure in a therapy group, assuming that the others had judged this "emotional lapse" as harshly as they themselves did.

CONTROL OVER FEELINGS

For many obsessives, control over their emotions is a crucial component of self-control. By their nature, emotions sometimes defy control, and this unruliness disturbs the obsessive. Also, through their extremist lenses, many obsessives unconsciously fear that any show of emotion could lead to their humiliating themselves, devastating someone else, being rejected, or even losing *all* self-control. For these and other reasons, many obsessives will repress, minimize, disown, or otherwise try to avoid strong emotions altogether.

Collette, for example, is a thirty-two-year-old pharmacist who, when she's angry at or hurt by someone, will evade rather than experience her feelings. One day Kay, another member of her therapy group, made a teasing comment about Collette's invariably flawless grooming. Collette at first appeared to ignore the veiled criticism, but when I interrupted to ask how Kay's comments had made her feel, she answered calmly, "I suppose I thought she has a right to her opinion, but I'm not about to change because of it."

"But what did you feel inside when she said it?" I persisted.

"It reminded me of my mother."

"And how does it feel when Kay says those things to you?"

"Well, it's like I'm being perfect . . . not letting down."

"When she talked about how every hair always seems to be in place, what were you feeling?"

"Maybe that she wants me to be something different." Suddenly Collette's eyes filled with tears. "That I'm not measuring up. She doesn't like me the way I am."

"And you are feeling . . ."

"Sad!"

When their feelings are starting to surface in therapy sessions, many obsessive patients like Collette will deliver an intellectual analysis of them, change the subject, joke, or focus on something trivial—anything to avoid actually *feeling* and exploring this perturbing part of themselves.

Selectively Unemotional

Although a few obsessives have difficulty showing *any* strong emotions (and thus may appear machinelike), most choke off only certain ones. Some, for instance, have no trouble showing affection, but can't display anger easily. With others, the opposite is true.

James was an attorney whom others found judgmental and aloof. He didn't hesitate to let other people know when he was annoyed or angry; in fact, his fierce persona was a professional asset. But James shrank from showing any hint of softness or vulnerability. One day in a group therapy session he was berating his parents, who had repeatedly disappointed him as a child, and had rarely shown him the warmth or approval he craved. As James bitterly described a recent encounter with them, another group member finally questioned why James couldn't let himself soften toward them, just a little.

James was silent for a while, then he replied, "If I do, I know they'll hurt me." He felt sure they would demonstrate once again their lack of caring for him, and would reject him. A fear of being vulnerable, engendered in his childhood, had driven him to keep strict control over his warm, affectionate feelings. But instead of protecting him, his self-control wound up hurting him terribly. No one would have guessed it from his smooth, cool demeanor, but one of his main complaints when he came to me initially was that he felt isolated and distanced from others, including his wife. His loneliness was causing him great pain, leading him to wonder if life was worth the struggle. Only the thought of his children made him push away thoughts of suicide.

James's mask did finally slip one day. In a discussion his eyes briefly filled with tears and his voice quivered for a moment. Although he quickly regained his composure, he felt deeply humiliated by this crack in his image. He thought the others would be repelled by his weakness, and he felt ashamed and frightened by the incident, although he couldn't articulate why.

In fact, it was at that moment that the other group members felt their first glimmer of warmth toward him. They previously had made it clear that they resented James's intimidating demeanor; his emotional detachment made it difficult to be relaxed and comfortable with him. They felt as if they were under a microscope—that James was observing and judging them without allowing himself to be vulnerable. And they pointed out, accurately, that his wife, child, and acquaintances must feel the same way.

So when tears welled up in his eyes, several people conveyed feelings of empathy and affection for him. Even though he could *intellectually* understand their positive reaction, it took time and many other interactions before James could integrate his insights into his everyday interpersonal behavior. Gradually he did succeed in showing his softer emotions and feeling less anxious about it. Whereas he and his wife had been prickly and guarded with each other, James slowly found himself more willing to reveal his fears and pain, as well as his love and need for her. In turn, *she* felt safer and able to be more open and vulnerable with him; their relationship steadily became more intimate and fulfilling.

The Downside of Emotional Control

To survive, work effectively, and relate to others harmoniously, we obviously must modulate some of our emotions. However, as James's experience illustrates, wholesale repression of feelings can be self-damaging. Even in moments of leisure or intimacy, many obsessives have difficulty shifting gears and letting go of their need to be in control. Some may repress their feelings so effectively that they do not know what their feelings are; they come to believe they were born without the normal emotional range present in others. This causes them pain, as they sense themselves to be defective in some core way.

In their wish to seem normal (to themselves and others), these people may fake whatever feelings they think are appropriate in various situations. Or they may unconsciously compensate for their perceived defect in an altogether different way, by idealizing it. Like *Star Trek*'s Mr. Spock, people who take this path disdain feelings as evidence of weakness. They sneer at emotional people and admire intellect and reason. They thus convert the pain of feeling defective into pride in being "strong."

Of course, such defensive tactics in obsessives usually are doomed to failure, because in spite of their best efforts, rage, terror, sadness, infatuation, and other emotions will eventually break through. Like anyone else, the obsessive person will experience these emotions because, fortunately, there is no *completely* effective anesthesia against feeling. Emotions are crucial components of who we are. And it is through expressing our emotions that we are able to make our needs known and achieve true communication with others. If you can't show that you're touched, hurt, scared, angry, or sad, people can't connect with you, let alone feel empathy for you or love you. In the emotional arena as in others, too much self-control is self-defeating.

Control Over Others

The second aspect of the Myth of Control is the need to control others. Often I can detect a new patient's efforts to control our relationship thirty seconds into our first phone conversation. In fact, the warning bells may have sounded even before then. Maybe the person initiates a game of "telephone tag"; he leaves word for me to call, but when I reach him, he asks if he can call me back in five minutes. Then he waits twenty, so that when he finally calls, I'm in session with another patient. Often we go a few more rounds before we actually speak. When we do, he may put me on the defensive, asking me questions about my qualifications or challenging my fee, subtly striving for the upper hand in our relationship. When I ask him questions, he may sidestep my queries and instead tell me things *he* thinks I should know about him. When we try to set up an appointment, he jockeys with me over an acceptable time.

People who have this quality make me think of flypaper. Interactions with them are sticky, somehow more complicated than those with other people.

In their quest to feel in control over others, they may take one of several different tacks. Most direct are those who rigidly insist that their employees, children, and spouses do things *their* way, never considering how such a dictatorial attitude makes other people feel. Like anyone else, these obsessives usually want others to view them as kind and nonjudgmental, and are surprised when they are not seen that way. They just can't bring themselves to do what it takes to win that reputation; they can't step back and let the people around them act in their own individual styles.

CONTROL THROUGH IRREPROACHABILITY

Far more commonly, however, my patients use a subtler strategy to control those around them: they strive to make people think well of them, always. The main objective underlying this strategy is to *leave no room for criticism.* In early childhood we learn which behaviors and abilities are labeled "good" by parents, teachers, and others. Many obsessives master these skills, developing a brilliant facility for identifying those attitudes and behaviors considered virtues in each new social setting, and then adopting them absolutely. Thoughts or impulses incompatible with this image of perfection are suppressed or rejected.

At thirty-four, Robert was married but had no children. He was sent to me by his internist because of anxiety, light-headedness, nausea, and palpitations that defied any medical diagnosis. Shortly after we met, he explained with a mixture of pride and self-disgust how he could quickly pick up on the "rules" of a situation, and conform to them flawlessly. As a result, he won approval from almost everyone.

At work he managed to be equally popular with his boss, his peers, and his subordinates. Among his acquaintances, Robert was a man of many faces. Athletic friends knew him as a keen sports fan and an athlete in his own right. With others who were academics, he presented himself as literate and intellectual. In each of these social systems he was in perfect sync, a model of the prevailing values, beyond criticism.

It would have astonished most of his friends to know that in spite of Robert's amazing capacity for adapting to the ground rules, he felt alienated, different from the others who, he assumed, really *did* belong. He was extraordinarily sensitive to others' opinions of him; whenever he even suspected that someone disapproved of something he had said or done, he felt anxious and would ruminate endlessly about the episode, seeking a way to somehow explain away or undo his perceived unfortunate comment or act. Coming up with such a solution was the only thing that would quell his anxiety.

On one occasion, for instance, he made a remark to a Hispanic colleague that he later thought might have sounded racist. This bothered him for days, until he finally set up a meeting with his co-worker to explain away what he had said as not really what he had meant. Ironically, his colleague didn't even remember Robert's comment, and was somewhat mystified by his elaborate rationalization.

In therapy, Robert and I explored situations like these over and over. We focused on how he was always trying to meet others' expectations, at a terrible emotional cost. Because he hated himself for what he perceived as weakness and phoniness, feelings of anxiety poisoned his every waking hour. Both at work and with friends in his leisure time, he felt constantly on the verge of "blowing it"; he thought a fall was inevitable if anyone was to get close enough to him for long enough. He even became tense about coming to therapy because he felt he'd started out as a star patient, articulate and insightful, but was about to reveal flaws and see my regard for him plummet. At such times, nausea and light-headedness could overwhelm him.

For Robert the easiest part of therapy was seeing how his perfect image was backfiring; much more difficult was putting that insight into practice. First, as is so often the case with obsessive patients, he had to practice something that comes quite easily to others: the art of knowing his own feelings. Many obsessives are truly bewildered when they're asked about their feelings. Often they're shocked to discover they have *any* feelings about a colleague or an event they've just described.

In order to make a true and full connection with others, Robert had to practice with me repeatedly before he began to know what he felt. Much of our work focused on helping him feel comfortable with his increased self-awareness, since he had always previously perceived his emotions to be dangerous (and his sense of self had come to rest partly on the *absence* from his conscious mind of jealousy, rage, dependency, or other such sentiments). As he slowly saw that *I* fully accepted him even when he showed these "bad" emotions, *he* became more able to accept them in himself as part of his identity. Only then was he ready for the second step.

He had to envision how he might have acted or spoken in various situations if he was being truly honest with himself and others. Then we examined together the likely reaction such a response would bring. Would others have rejected him? Lost respect for him? Reevaluated him as "just average"? Little by little, Robert tried to incorporate more "authentic" behavior into his everyday life. I urged him to go slowly, gently voicing an unpopular (but truly held) dissident opinion here, admitting ignorance or permitting himself a less-than-perfect performance there. We especially worked on such things as improving his ability to say no to unwelcome additional responsibilities—even to his boss. Therapists call this "setting limits."

Robert did experience anxiety during this period, especially when he found himself a bit less universally admired, but he also found out that the sky didn't fall when he allowed himself to be more genuine and less perfect. As he gradually stopped hating himself for his phoniness, he became better able to let people get close. When someone liked him, he knew it wasn't because of some role he was playing, so he trusted that person's positive response more. He was no longer as afraid of exposure. The more genuine his relationships seemed to him, the more his anxiety around people began to recede.

Like other aspects of the control myth, trying to control other people's feelings by being wonderful has major drawbacks. For one thing, it's impossible. You simply can't embody *everyone's* idea of virtue. Anyone who tries to do so is bound to incur someone's disapproval sooner or later. And when the obsessive can't prevent someone from being angry with him, rejecting him, or doubting his abilities or character, he may find it impossible to let it go. Often he'll ruminate about the incident, unable to relax, until he devises a way to "fix" it.

Trying to stay above criticism is furthermore harmful because the constant self-betrayal it requires weakens such would-be paragons' sense of identity. It also throws them into conflict; if they can't tolerate any disapproval, how can they also be a perfectly honest person, strong and uncompromising in their values?

CONTROL GAMES

Subtly manipulative control games are another way in which obsessives strive to assert their power over others. Such power plays whisper: "I've got the upper hand here. I decide whether or not we will interact. And if we do, I decide the beginning, ending, and content of those interactions." Note that I say *whisper;* you very well may not recognize that you're the object of such tactics. In fact the obsessive himself usually is not conscious that he's doing it. Part of the nature of these ploys is that each has an alternate, perfectly reasonable explanation. When your colleague shows up several minutes late for a meeting, it may well be that a last-minute phone call unavoidably delayed her. But when this happens repeatedly, you have to wonder if her slight tardiness doesn't spring from an unconscious need to demonstrate that *she,* and not other people, decides when she's got to be somewhere.

You might sense a similar obstructionism in a variety of situations. Perhaps you've learned that a certain friend invariably wanders away from or lags behind the rest of the group on outings, forcing you all to search or wait for him. Or the checker behind the register in the grocery store somehow seems to sense your impatience—and you could swear that in response she *slows down,* almost imperceptibly. For a fleeting moment you taste a contest of wills in which the other person must demonstrate her dominance.

The tactic of making another person wait can assume a variety of guises. It may involve prolonging a decision. Perhaps you need to know what your spouse is planning for Friday evening, so you can decide whether you're free to attend a professional meeting. But your spouse just can't seem to come to a decision, leaving you stymied.

Or a friend or co-worker may make you wait before successfully connecting on the phone. "Can I call you right back?" they'll invariably ask. Eventually, you may begin to sense that they need to call back not because they're (always) busy, but because they're uncomfortable unless they're the one initiating the contact.

Along the same lines, certain patients insist upon having the last word in our meetings. When I make a comment such as, "Well, I see our time is up. We have to stop now," at an unconscious level this is a frightening and humiliating reminder that I control some aspects of our relationship. So they stand up as if to depart, but at the door they might start a social conversation, or give me an "assignment," reminding me to ask my secretary for a certain form, for instance. Such behaviors serve to soothe patients' anxiety by letting them feel at least some control over the ending of a session and our relationship in general.

All these interpersonal control tactics do accomplish their aim to a degree. However, their net result is often painful and destructive, because ultimately they obstruct the sense of connection and intimacy that all humans need and crave.

Control over Life's Impersonal Events

Besides self-control and control over others, the third component of the Myth of Control says that *if one is sufficiently cautious and vigilant, it is possible to guard against such impersonal dangers as illness, accidents, economic upheavals, and so on.*

Being sufficiently cautious and vigilant may mean staying abreast of events that could have personal ramifications—from the weather to political issues to the latest medical news. Obsessives believe that knowledge imparts a protective power. A related form of "vigilance" is the obsessive's tendency to worry, as if internal fretting over anything that might go wrong can actually prevent it from happening.

A preoccupation with organization is another way some obsessives create an illusion of control. They may go to extremes to impose order and predictability upon their lives, avoiding the unknown and steering away from risky enterprises, as if these measures will forestall unexpected misfortune.

When obsessives can't tell how an event might affect them and also can't avoid or prevent it, they may adopt a self-protective pessimism. Before an annual evaluation at work, they might predict to a colleague that their review will be poor. They might complain that they haven't had time to get all their projects in good shape, and that the boss doesn't like them and will be sure to ambush them over some minor detail. In this way they set themselves up to "win" even if their evaluation does turn out badly. Prediction of a mishap runs a close second to preventing it; it provides at least an illusion of control.

THE COSMIC SCOREKEEPER

Many obsessives quell their anxiety about life's possible catastrophes in still another way. At an unconscious level they convince themselves

27

that terrible things will not happen to them simply because *life is fair.*

This conviction, though deeply buried and therefore unspoken, is crucial to obsessives. They can't bear to face the reality that they are at least somewhat at the mercy of such haphazard or uncontrollable forces as accidents, illness, and the peculiarities of others. Facing this fact would be terrifying because to the obsessive's all-or-nothing way of thinking, imperfect protection is the same as *no* protection at all.

Their "fairness doctrine" helps them to hold on to the illusion of control. And intertwined with the conviction of cosmic justice, most obsessives hold a belief, also unconscious, in what I call the Cosmic Scorekeeper. The Scorekeeper may dovetail with a belief in an established religion, but I've also seen plenty of atheists with the unconscious faith that an omnipresent, omnipotent force assesses and reconciles the score, thus ensuring that people get what they deserve. This notion enables obsessives to believe that they can control their destiny by being good or bad.

They can guarantee themselves safe passage by making the Scorekeeper *owe* it to them. They do this by piling up a track record of self-denial, sacrifice, industry, diligence, honesty, and loyalty rivaling that of a saint. They try to avoid behaviors, feelings, even thoughts that will subtract points from their stockpile of sacrifices. They avoid selfishness, lust, dishonesty, laziness, hedonism. Even enjoying themselves costs them points!

Before doing something "selfish," they may need to earn it by performing some distasteful (but noble) duty. They might put in extra overtime at work, or undertake an unpleasant home-repair project. Such sacrifices increase the debt owed them by the Scorekeeper. With a huge positive balance, they might even be able to take a vacation or spend money on a personal indulgence without bankrupting their account.

What happens should the obsessive blunder into "unearned" enjoyment? When Dory's section chief suddenly decided to send her to a conference in Rome, she felt anxious after her initial elation. At an unconscious level, she was anticipating some score-evening blow. To blunt the threat, she piled up "sacrifice points" by working overtime as much as possible in the short time before the trip. Then she almost sabotaged her good fortune by finding reasons to avoid going. When she finally went, she had difficulty enjoying herself. Like many other obsessives, every time things begin to go "too well" for her, Dory braces herself for the Scorekeeper to balance them out.

Similarly, if she has some bad luck, she wonders what she did to cause it. Did she step on the figurative crack in the sidewalk? Did she have overly selfish or hostile thoughts? Did she feel too much pleasure? Or let herself become too optimistic and confident, jinxing herself? The minute she finds her "misstep," she feels better because she can tell herself that she can prevent the misfortune next time by simply behaving differently.

Obsessives tend to judge other people's lives by the same standard of fairness. They feel no compassion when they hear of mishaps befalling those they consider unworthy or "bad," and they resent it when honors or other good fortune come to someone "undeserving."

They themselves often seem as intent upon *trying* to accomplish various tasks as upon actually accomplishing them. They expect the Scorekeeper to compensate them for good intentions and for effort regardless of results. And if they work at something such as school, therapy, or staying healthy, and their efforts don't succeed, they may feel cheated and resentful.

If, as is so common, the obsessive has been a decent, conscientious, honest person and has consistently denied himself many pleasures in life, he will have earned IOUs by the thousands. And yet the chances are his life still contains plenty of rough spots: He has to work hard; he gets ill several times a year; less deserving people all around him are becoming more famous or rich; his financial investments haven't always panned out; not everyone likes him or appreciates what a good person he is; and he often feels unhappy or depressed.

He may become bitter about all this, as if he's been misled by the Scorekeeper or betrayed by life in general. If he suffers a major personal setback, the result can be a blinding rage.

For Helen, the blow came when Jack, her husband of ten years, told her that he intended to marry another, younger woman. With that, he packed and moved out to live with his lover. As anyone might expect, Helen felt a gamut of incredibly painful emotions: betrayal, humiliation, disappointment, loss, sadness, inadequacy, and a sense of failure. As the intensity of these feelings began to diminish, what came to the surface was rage. Predictably, Helen felt angry at Jack and his new lover, but she was also angry about *something else* that at first she couldn't articulate.

Only gradually was she able to recognize the source of this rage. Helen had grown up with the unconscious conviction that if you are a kind, loyal, and supportive friend or spouse, the Scorekeeper will see to it that these attitudes are reciprocated. Throughout the years of her marriage, it became increasingly clear that Jack wasn't particularly concerned about Helen's well-being, or interested in her thoughts, feelings, or day-to-day life, even though she tried desperately to please him. But because her sense of safety in the world depended so much on keeping intact her fairness myth, she couldn't allow herself to see her marriage clearly. She had to blind herself to the imbalances in their relationship. Also, acknowledging her husband's shortcomings and unfairness toward her would have brought to the surface anger that she believed would have threatened the relationship, and she was too emotionally dependent on the marriage to risk this.

This long-suppressed rage finally erupted when Jack walked out. Eventually Helen was able literally to shout at me that she couldn't stand the *unfairness* of what had happened to her! She had been faithful to him, sensitive, kind, generous, supportive—and none of it had stopped him from betraying her. She couldn't accept that all the good-faith effort in the world on her part had not protected her one bit; that nothing she could have done would have *guaranteed* her safety from this misfortune. She had to face the devastating fact that her Scorekeeper was a figment.

Despite this insight, Helen still continued to act in her old pattern. She would accommodate Jack on the time and place for their property-settlement discussions, tolerating his tardiness and his changing the meeting times. Invariably Jack would take advantage of her generosity, disregarding her schedule, ignoring her pain, and even unlawfully entering her home. And each time Helen would wind up in a rage over the *unfairness* of Jack's behavior. Time after time she expected fairness and was disappointed and outraged when she failed to get it.

The supreme unfairness was that he, the unfaithful one, was having a great time, had a loving relationship, a new home, and most of the money, while she—the giving, faithful, fair one—wound up isolated, despairing, and stuck with most of the bills.

Over time Helen and I again and again confronted her expectation of fairness, and gradually she began to see how she was setting herself up for disappointment and constant rage. She also began to see how placing her fate in the hands of the Scorekeeper prevented her from acting in her own behalf to take care of herself. For example, she had been unable to bring herself to hire an attorney.

Helen gradually became able to relinquish her notion of a Cosmic Scorekeeper and to change her behavior accordingly. She stopped expecting Jack to be fair to her, for example—and discovered she was able to handle him much more effectively. She also hired a good attorney and put effort into helping him.

She continued to feel angry, but her anger was more reasonable, based on specific issues and not on outrage over the unfairness of life. And incidentally, as she underwent this change, Jack began to find her more attractive. From time to time he even sounded her out about possibly getting back together again. As things turned out, Helen was the one to terminate what she came to see as an unhealthy relationship.

Control Strategies Can Conflict

We've seen how the obsessive's need for control extends into three main areas: control of self, others, and impersonal events. Although I have discussed each separately, these three aspects of control often commingle. Sometimes they conflict.

Jennifer, for instance, recounted this sequence of events. She was a perfectionist with strong opinions about everything from what dish detergent worked best to which clothing designers offered the best buy for the money. So when she and a group of friends were deciding where to go for dinner, Jennifer knew immediately in her own mind which was the best choice. She refrained, however, from explicitly trying to persuade the group to go there. "I didn't want the whole decision to be on my shoulders," she said. (In the next chapters we'll take a close look at how perfectionism commonly provokes such fear of decision-making.) Instead she insisted that the choice made no difference to her. The more the group discussed other possibilities, however, the more Jennifer inwardly chafed. Almost in spite of herself, she began to try unobtrusively to influence the decision toward her preference, casually mentioning a few advantages of the spot, noting a drawback to one of the alternatives. And yet almost the moment the group did select her preference, Jennifer found herself regretting she had ever said anything that might have tipped the scales in the decision. All the way to the restaurant she worried: about whether the same chef was working there; whether everyone in the group would like this type of food; whether the service would be too slow. Later, when one of her companions voiced a minor complaint about his meal, the comment deeply upset her. She had assumed total responsibility over the whole experience, as if it were within her control to make everything work out well.

She didn't have any such control, of course, nor would she consciously have claimed that she did. Yet her attitude and actions reveal a complex mix of controlling tactics. Her desire to control the group's behavior directly (by picking the restaurant outright) conflicted with her fear that her choice might turn out to be less than perfect, and thus lower her friends' opinion of her. When she nonetheless subtly nudged them into selecting her choice, she began to worry (as if that might prevent the worst from happening) and to voice some of her concerns in a display of self-protective pessimism.

Failure of the Myth

A whole host of experiences stand ready to contradict the Myth of Control, pointing out to obsessives that in fact they *can't* always completely control themselves, others, and life's impersonal events. They will feel some irrepressible emotions and see their self-discipline lapse at times. Despite their best efforts, someone at some time is bound to disapprove of them. And despite all their precautions and all their attempts to mollify the Scorekeeper, obsessives, like anyone else, are almost certain to get sick, hurt themselves, or suffer financial reverses now and then.

RETROACTIVE CONTROL

When the obsessive's control fails in one of these ways, a flood of anxiety will surface, unless she can ignore or distort what has happened. One common "fudge factor" is what I call Retroactive Control. The words "should've," "could've," or "would've" are essential for this. She should've done this instead of that. If only she had, she would've been better off. She could've struck it rich, avoided the flu, or performed better.

Using this trick enables the obsessive to recast the frightening events *after* they happen. It offers him a possible escape route from the truth—that one's control over life is frequently imperfect at best. Should he catch a cold, he immediately searches for, and usually finds, a good reason: a draft he "should've" avoided, too little sleep, forgetting to take his normal dose of vitamins.

Even when it would have been impossible for them to act differently, I see people who insist that they not only could have, but should have done so. I remember a very control-oriented man who was just devastated by his girlfriend's refusal to return to the relationship after finding a new boyfriend.

Interestingly, Dennis insisted that she'd left him because of things he did or didn't do, and that he would readily do these things differently (and thus save the relationship) if only she would give him another chance. But I learned that Dennis's recollection of the relationship was seriously distorted. His ex-girlfriend had voiced several legitimate reasons for wanting to break up, and most of them were unrelated to his behavior toward her. (She couldn't reconcile their religious differences, for one thing. She also was uncomfortable with the fact that Dennis was fifteen years older than she.) Yet Dennis adamantly denied that these were her true objections to the relationship. It became clear that his stubborn insistence stemmed from his need to cling to some sense of retroactive control. As long as he could blame the breakup on things he *did,* he could have chosen to do them differently. He couldn't accept the fact that she had left because of things that were totally out of *anyone's* control. Acknowledging this would have meant acknowledging also that the Myth of Control was just that—a myth. His anxiety would have soared.

WHEN EVEN RETROACTIVE CONTROL FAILS

Despite the usefulness of Retroactive Control in reducing the obsessive's anxiety, life presents many catastrophes that cannot be denied or erased by any psychological sleight of hand. Such an event happened in San Diego, where I practice, on a September morning in 1978.

On that day a Boeing 727 filled with 135 people was making a routine descent into Lindbergh Field, when it collided with a single-engine Cessna flown by a student pilot and his instructor. The small plane disintegrated instantly, but the crippled airliner remained intact as it plunged to the ground. The tragedy monopolized the local news media for days. I continued to see the impact of the tragedy for months, however, as some of my obsessive patients wrestled with severe feelings of anxiety.

They couldn't dispel images of how the passengers in the plane had had utterly no control over their destinies and had to face the inevitability of their doom for the twenty to thirty seconds that the plane was plunging downward. More than any other aspect of the crash, it was the idea of that helpless half-minute that was so intolerable to these patients.

My patients couldn't ignore the knowledge that they themselves could easily have been passengers on that plane (a routine commuter flight from Sacramento). Not being on the flight was clearly a result of pure chance. They couldn't give themselves the usual myth-saving reassurances like "I would never ride in a private plane," or "I would never fly during a storm," or "I would never travel in a country during a civil war." The tragedy made them confront their own inescapable mortality.

The anxiety they felt was an inevitable consequence of having seen their control mythology shaken. The whole reason obsessives construct and embrace the Myth of Control is to fend off anxiety; and when an experience contradicts the myth, if they can't ignore or reinterpret the experience, that anxiety returns with a vengeance. They may even develop physical symptoms such as headaches, stomach problems, sleeplessness, or dizzy spells.

But even when they aren't acutely suffering, obsessives' rigid need for control is causing them irreparable damage. Their much-vaunted self-control, for example, is like some impervious suit of armor that has rusted shut and can no longer be shed. Fashioned in childhood as protection, it has become life-constricting. Their rigidly controlled posture has in itself become a source of pride that they're terrified of jeopardizing. And though they long to be more easygoing, flexible, and spontaneous, fear inhibits them.

That fear is one of the reasons why change is particularly difficult for obsessives, even those who are suffering deeply as a result of this self-imposed control. There are other reasons as well, which will become clear in the course of this book. Yet despite the many impediments, I believe you can make significant beneficial changes if you are armed with two things: motivation and insight.

By motivation I mean a willingness and a desire to put consistent effort into changing the attitudes and behaviors that are causing some of your unhappiness. By insight I mean an understanding of exactly how your particular obsessive traits are causing you harm, and some ideas for alternative attitudes and behaviors. Though I will offer you frequent encouragement, the motivation for change must come from within. Your insight, on the other hand, should be greatly enhanced by the following chapters, which provide an in-depth look at the most important obsessive traits. We begin with the driven quest for perfection.

THREE

Too Perfect

Whoever thinks a faultless
piece to see
Thinks what ne'er was, nor is,
nor e'er shall be.

    —ALEXANDER POPE,
An Essay on Criticism

Let's say that doing a good job is important to you. You try to avoid making mistakes. You pay attention to detail and strive to be thorough. You value competence, both in yourself and in others. Does this mean you're a perfectionist?

Not necessarily. The attributes I just described are all aspects of a normal, healthy *will to excel,* a personality trait that can help one achieve personal satisfaction, material success, and professional recognition. But in some people the will to excel takes on exaggerated proportions. Such people harbor the unconscious conviction that any mistake at all is completely unacceptable. They are driven to seek not just excellence but perfection. At an unconscious level, perfectionists believe that *mistake-free living is both possible and urgently necessary.*

The Perfectionist's Credo says:

1. If I always try my very best and if I'm alert and sharp enough, I can avoid error. Not only can I perform flawlessly in everything important and be the ideal person in every situation, but I can avoid everyday blunders, oversights, and poor decisions or choices.

2. It's crucial to avoid making mistakes because they would show that I'm not as competent as I should be.

3. By being perfect, I can ensure my own security with others. They will admire me and will have no reason to criticize or reject me. They could not prefer anyone else to me.

4. My worth depends on how "good" I am, how smart I am, and how well I perform.

Perfection and Control Overlap

If you examine this credo closely, you'll see that, as with the Myth of Control, it is an unconscious device for quelling anxieties. It results from a child's fanciful *attempt to guarantee his security among others and his sense of adequacy by excelling, and generally leaving no room for criticism.* The child destined to become a perfectionist views perfection as the only fail-safe way to ensure that he won't be vulnerable to such dangers as criticism, embarrassment, anger, or the withdrawal of love by his parents and others.

Being perfect and leaving no room for criticism is also one of the ways in which the obsessive wields control in his relationships. And control and perfection can go hand in hand in other ways. Being morally perfect, for example, is one way to keep the Cosmic Scorekeeper in one's debt.

Just as with the control myth, protecting and confirming the Perfectionist's Credo is crucial to the obsessive's mental equilibrium. To the strongly perfectionistic obsessive, being wrong is not just the everyday occurrence that most of us shrug off—it's a psychic disaster. "I just can't stumble," patient after patient has told me. "Every small failure is devastating."

Failures are devastating because they jeopardize the Credo and thus trigger anxiety. Also, the perfectionist comes to base a lot of his self-esteem and pride on being able to do things flawlessly, so errors make him feel stupid or inadequate. He's also likely to become quite angry with himself—proof that he believes he should have been able to avoid the error. If the error or fault is seen by another, he may feel embarrassed. Many obsessives seem to sense a constant, ever-lurking threat of embarrassment or humiliation, and they will go to great lengths to avoid it.

Perfectionism Versus the Will to Excel

It's important to distinguish between perfectionism and a healthy will to excel, which is a reasoned desire to perform competently. The latter is flexible and reasonable, while perfectionism is self-defeating, rigid, and driven. While the healthy achiever usually takes intrinsic pleasure in doing a job well, making good decisions, and having his excellence recognized, he keeps a rational perspective. He realizes that some tasks don't allow much room for error; if he happens to be a surgeon or a pilot, he takes the time to plan and prepare for his professional tasks and then carries them out in an exacting, thorough manner, with total attention to detail. On the other hand, when he's preparing dinner for company or choosing a shirt, he can be far less exacting. Unlike the perfectionist, he realizes that in these matters an error won't have major consequences and they don't warrant a lot of worry. He usually can enjoy himself with even a less than perfect outcome.

THE SUBJECTIVE EXPERIENCE OF ACHIEVEMENT

Even when the perfectionist and his healthier counterpart carry out a given activity equally flawlessly, they often differ in their subjective experience of that accomplishment. A healthy will to excel tends to bring one pleasure, while perfectionism quite often is a source of pain. One patient who had played the piano in childhood and returned to it as an adult described how her own perfectionistic expectations were taking the pleasure out of her studies. "I find myself feeling tense even when I'm alone, practicing. I worry that I'm not making progress fast enough. I know that I have an aptitude for music, and other people would say I play well. But I never feel that I've mastered anything. Even when I really know a piece, hitting a few wrong notes tends to ruin it for me."

The non-perfectionist doesn't need to be right all the time. His security doesn't depend upon having a spotless record or being viewed as the ideal person. But when he does achieve a goal or overcome an obstacle, he feels gratification, fulfillment, even joy.

The perfectionist, on the other hand, is apt to experience any given task or interaction as a test that will reflect his adequacy. So it's always important for him to do things correctly, know the answer, make the "right" decision. His goal and motives in any endeavor are so complicated that he can hardly avoid being preoccupied and tense. When he does achieve excellence, he can rarely enjoy it.

Every day I see the cost exacted by this illusory ideal of perfection. If you have to be flawlessly competent at practically everything, even the least significant of life's tasks can be transformed into a nightmare. One patient in her thirties described for me the stresses involved in planning her nine-year-old daughter's birthday party:

"I feel I have to do such a good job of everything; it's very hard for me to stop trying to improve various details. Last night, for instance, I thought up a new idea for party favors that would fit in beautifully with the theme of the party. It'll be quite a bit of work. But I just can't seem to draw the line. I keep feeling that if every aspect of the party doesn't turn out perfectly, the whole party will be a flop, as crazy as that sounds. I have the sense that people will think less of me.

"It takes the fun out of everything! I can't enjoy anything because I'm too worried about making sure it's just right."

Performance Pitfalls

Besides putting many obsessives under enormous pressure, the Perfectionist's Credo can cause other insidious damage. It often propels obsessives into self-defeating behaviors that far outweigh the rewards of avoiding errors.

DEADLY DEADLINES

Many perfectionists chronically have trouble getting their work done, or even started. They tend to procrastinate because all tasks loom large when they have to be done flawlessly.

"I have to force myself to do anything," a city planner named Stephen told me. "For example, in writing reports, I can make a quick decision as to what recommendation is appropriate—and I usually know it would hold up in the long run. My judgment is good. But when it comes down to actually making the recommendations, I'll put it off. I'm afraid I'll be *judged* for what I'm recommending."

Once a task is undertaken, the perfectionist always finds room for improvement. No matter how much time he spends on a project, there's always the chance someone will catch an incomplete or erroneous detail. So he holds on to it, spending far more time than necessary. In his mind, the danger is in letting go of something before it is truly perfect. Under this pressure, some perfectionists actually miss their deadlines, while others meet them but pay a terrible personal cost.

I've seen some remarkable examples of just how long people will cling to "almost-finished" tasks rather than letting go. I remember one economist who became mired in perfectionist behavior each time he wrote a paper for a scientific conference. To "cover" himself, he would polish and revise his writing until it was too late to take the chance of mailing the document. Then he would actually fly to the city of the conference to hand-deliver his submission on the day of the deadline— still furiously revising it on the plane!

I was even more struck by the case of one forty-year-old graduate student who had been working for several years on just the *introduction* to her dissertation. Leona had already been turned down for one job at a first-rate university because she had made so little progress on her writing.

"I keep taking more notes, making more outlines," she told me, "but I don't actually write. When I come up with an idea, rather than just write it out, I'll look for more material to make the idea more profound. Yet I realize that my best ideas come from writing, rather than from outlining and taking notes."

"Then why aren't you doing that?" I asked.

After a long pause she replied, "I'm not sure. I feel paralyzed by the pressure to produce something better on this topic than anything that has already been written."

"Why does it have to be *better?*"

"I think about the reactions of those who will review my work. I'm especially worried about one professor who has been a big supporter of mine. I imagine his reading it and realizing that I'm not as talented as he thought."

This patient wanted every sentence to be profound, and she couldn't write down a single word until she was absolutely certain it was the *right* word. Ironically, the longer the writing took, the higher she felt others' expectations would be, so the self-imposed pressure mounted with each passing month.

Over and over, I've heard patients describe being frozen into inaction by the awesome imperative to do a task not just perfectly, but in a way that truly impresses or astounds—in other words, to be "great." I have to stress that most of the time the obsessive doesn't walk around consciously thinking that he or she must tower above other people; acknowledged consciously, it sounds pretentious. But whenever I question, point by point, why she can't afford an oversight in her presentation or why he can't stand to be seen as an average attorney (or designer, or chef, or teacher), a submerged desire to astound people with his or her knowledge or ability emerges.

Not only can the imperative to be great inhibit one's day-to-day functioning, but it can also, paradoxically, discourage one from developing one's talents—sometimes at a tragically early age. I think of Janine, a gifted twenty-seven-year-old architect who consistently had trouble undertaking important projects because she was convinced she had to "produce a design so innovative that it stands everyone on their ears." Even sadder was Janine's outlook for her future. "I had so many plans, so many fantasies," she told me. "But because my work has to be so incredibly good, it takes infinitely longer to *execute* something than to simply think of doing it. I feel like I've wasted the last two years. Anything I do now will be less than what I fantasized I would do. So now it feels like there's no use."

THE COMPLETION COMPLEX

A trait related to the need to be flawless is the need to be *thorough.* Bowing to this pressure when preparing a presentation or written report, the perfectionist will include far more information than necessary. He can't draw the line between what is and isn't important, and he can't risk leaving anything out for fear someone will think he wasn't fully informed. What if he loses the sale (or the case or the grant) because of one small omission? Or what if this leads to his doing increasingly sloppy work and he winds up being just average?

Among countless examples of this behavior, one is provided by the teacher who feels driven to give the perfect lecture. She fastidiously presents reams of background information, but then finds herself having to rush through the very issues to which she was building. In fact, her students often can't follow her increasingly frantic lectures and walk out without having absorbed the main point.

Another example is that of the doctor who takes an unnecessarily exhaustive medical history from his new patient, then gives a very thorough physical exam, only to find himself behind schedule. With more and more patients waiting, he writes out a hasty prescription and gives the patient only the briefest instructions for taking the medicine. The patient walks out feeling badly handled.

Sometimes, when I ask an obsessive patient about one specific point—such as "Have you been sleeping well lately?"—he'll bombard me with much more detail than I need. Experience has taught me that if I try to short-circuit the responses to get the information I want, he's apt to get annoyed with me for crowding or rushing him. So his answer monopolizes our conversation—and we wind up having to cram our discussion of the more important issues into the final minutes of our session.

Bear in mind that several unconscious motives may shape a person's behavior in this type of situation. Filling the room with details and lengthy explanations also enables a therapy patient to avoid confronting his feelings. Yet another covert motive may be to keep me in a listening rather than a pressing, intruding mode. (If he's leading the discussion, he's wielding the reins, not I.)

However, the obsessive's chief motive for covering topics in such fine detail is usually his exaggerated fear of omitting something that will turn out to be important. This fear blinds the person to the fact that too much detail can dull the impact of his main points, boring and confusing listeners rather than clarifying. If every base has to be touched and all pros, cons, and caveats acknowledged, communication is sterile. It lacks color, force, and focus. Perfectionism once again winds up detracting from overall performance, rather than enhancing it.

Physical Clutter

Just as some perfectionists' speech is cluttered with too much detail, others have trouble discarding *things* in their lives. They are crippled by the fear that they may make an irreversible error in throwing something away, and by their inability to prioritize.

One of the most extreme examples I've ever seen of this involved a fifty-year-old hospital administrator named Karl. When I met him, Karl had been living in his apartment for almost two years, yet boxes and packing crates were piled four to six feet high, filling most of the living space. Though Karl had arranged a neat path between them to connect the various rooms, so little space was left that he had almost no furniture. He even slept on the floor!

He told me that the boxes contained newspapers, magazines, and books he planned to read "as soon as I get the time." Nor could he discard old letters, broken tools, or empty containers because "you never know when something will come in handy." Of course, Karl couldn't invite people to his apartment, where they would see the appalling clutter, so his social life foundered. Yet each time he decided that he had to discard *something,* he was overwhelmed by the pressure of prioritizing; somehow everything seemed equally important.

His abhorrence of errors was also choking off his productivity at work, and even affected his style of speech. For fear of leaving out any detail that might prove important, Karl got bogged down in rambling, over-inclusive monologues that even he could see were off-putting.

45

When I asked why he couldn't at least put the boxes in storage, he offered one feeble rationalization after another: he said he might need something from one of the boxes, and it would be inconvenient to retrieve it if they were in storage. He was also unsure which was the best storage facility, and needed more information before making up his mind.

The more I pressed him, however, the more Karl was willing to face the implications of all his rationalizations. One day he admitted that instead of holding on to his piles of magazines he *could* go to the library to look up magazine references. On another occasion he suddenly remembered an old television program featuring the Milquetoast high school teacher named Mr. Peepers. In this particular episode, Mr. Peepers was trying to persuade his students to memorize the formula for sulfuric acid by warning them that the President of the United States might someday pop in on them. How would they feel if the President asked them for the formula and they didn't know it? Karl smiled ruefully when he recounted his memory of the show—but he was also admitting to a similarly twisted logic that was still influencing, indeed paralyzing, his own life.

Fortunately, Karl had reached the point where his stagnation had become so unbearable that he was willing to risk making some changes. He learned to remind himself of the costs of his perfectionism. Little by little he began approving work charts even when they lacked some tiny, nonessential bit of information. This cut down the backlog in which he was drowning. And he finally plunged in and began to weed through some of the junk that filled his apartment. Almost immediately he began to feel relief; seeing clearly how his self-protective perfectionism had been undermining him helped him resist and overcome it.

As we'll see in chapter 8, some obsessives go to the opposite extreme; they're too orderly. But milder variations of Karl's disorderliness are common in obsessives. They might generally be sloppy, or the

a mistake be absolutely undeniable, they may still have
ımly acknowledging their error. Often they will become
tossing off so many *buts*, *howevers*, and other qualifications
listeners can barely hear the admission within the verbal
ven in admitting error, perfectionists seem to be saying that
. . . semi-right. Somehow they make it appear that, given
nstances, being slightly in error was the most intelligent
 have taken. Throughout, they fail to notice how repelled
 be by this stubborn pretense at infallibility.

ir need to be above criticism, perfectionistic obsessives may
 convince a hurt or angry friend that his feelings are inap-
or "wrong." I've seen this in parents interacting with their
The parent will point out an error and the child will defend
bviously hurt by the criticism. The parent, instead of ac-
ing the child's feelings, responds by pointing out more rea-
 the criticism was *accurate,* implying that the child has no
be hurt. The child winds up feeling bad not only because
a mistake and because he was criticized by this powerful fig-
also because he was "wrong" to have been wounded by the

same kind of interaction commonly unfolds between teacher
ent, between husband and wife, or between colleagues. One
ill blurt out to the other, "You shouldn't feel that way!" In
e the obsessive may be surprised when the other person feels
 still further after being proved "wrong" for feeling a certain
 obsessive fails to see the damage done by trying to transform
 of feelings into a debate: all too often it pushes the other
nto keeping future complaints to himself while smoldering
e surface. But, given the way obsessives tend to downplay
 it's not surprising that they would act as if the weight of logic
uld banish the hurt and angry feelings of a loved one.

---

disorder may be confined to one area of their lives—to their car, say, or to one particular closet. In many cases the ironic underlying cause of the mess is perfectionism. Cleaning up would require scrubbing every surface, removing every molecule of dust, finding a place to store every possession, a task so herculean that it would daunt anyone.

Not-So-Perfect Relationships

The most serious effects of perfectionism can be seen in personal relationships. Such problems spring from

- the fear of having other people see one's flaws
- the need to be right about everything
- a constantly critical attitude

SOCIAL INHIBITIONS

Let's look first at the fear of letting other people see one's shortcomings. This fear is responsible for a variety of social inhibitions that can range in intensity from slight apprehension to full-blown terror, complete with pounding heartbeat, weakness, upset stomach, and other symptoms.

Marian felt the noxious impact of her perfectionistic fear when she decided to join a walking club for exercise. She drove to the meeting place at the appointed time, parked, and then couldn't bring herself to join the group. The thought of how "funny" she looked in her new walking shorts literally paralyzed her, and her sudden light-headedness and shakiness further upset her. She couldn't face the mortifying possibility that her nervousness might be so obvious she would have to excuse herself. Bitterly disappointed, she drove home again.

Social fears may be subtle. Say you begin learning a foreign language, just for pleasure. When you stumble over words and grammar, instead of simply accepting such mistakes as an inevitable part of the process, you feel embarrassed and humiliated, and may eventually abandon the study. Ultimately you restrict yourself to those few endeavors in which you feel competent, closing off potentially enriching or enjoyable experiences. A clear majority of my obsessive patients tell me regretfully of things they never allowed themselves to do, though they wanted to very badly.

Many obsessives view dating and sex as a graded performance—one fraught with the threat of criticism or unfavorable comparisons. Many adolescent obsessives shrink from romantic encounters rather than risk appearing foolish or showing their ignorance. Consequently they have less social and sexual experience than their peers, which makes them feel increasingly inept. The cycle continues, with isolation and loneliness the usual result.

While the form of the specific fear may vary widely, *most socially inhibited people harbor distorted fears of being noticed and having their flaws exposed.* The vast majority feel themselves to be under scrutiny much more than is the case, and they believe that others will reject them or will respect them less if any slips or imperfections show through. One woman, for example, told me about going out for a walk one evening and coming upon a line of people waiting to see a movie. The thought of being watched by all those people was so unbearable that she elected to walk all the way around the block rather than pass by them. Another patient became overwhelmed by feelings of anxiety in any group of people; even grocery shopping would trigger strange spells of feeling as if his face were "cracking." Still another, a brilliant physicist, suffered from such intense stage fright that any public presentation made him perspire profusely, which of course made him feel even more self-conscious.

None of these people could readily explain their enormous and paralyzing vulnerability; the underlying irrational ideas that perpetuate

social fears usually aren't obvious. |
and inhibition is all too clear. Asid
live with, you find yourself missing
ment, and the ability to enjoy peo

BEING RIGHT—AT ALL COSTS

A different way in which perfection
ships stems from the perfectionistic
thing. Errors are anathema to the pe
sometimes. (After all, perfectionism
not be mistake-free.) Lots of obsessi
that they make mistakes. Being able
is, after all, part of being "the perfec
istic obsessives tend to avoid owning
in important matters, and this often

It's simply unpleasant to be aroun
show he was right. For one thing, you
input if the other person has to act as
And you can't teach anything to someo
tacitly that his understanding was eve

This inability often emerges in the
other group members make an observati
common for him to resist it or say that it
into a long-winded explication of the po
the original comment. It makes the obs
simply weren't heard.

Perfectionists often try to talk their
they gently hammer away at their oppor
ers back down, if just from fatigue. Or
position was misunderstood. They nimbly
culpability.

Should
trouble ca
defensive,
that their
thicket. E
they were
the circu
position t
others ca

In the
even try t
propriate
children.
himself,
knowledg
sons why
right to
he made
ure, but
critique.

The
and stud
person v
each cas
alienate
way. Th
a sharin
person
under t
feelings
alone c

Pickiness

The type of perfectionism in which the perfectionist himself is the subject of scrutiny is perhaps the most obvious. But there is another variation of perfectionism: an exaggerated inclination to be upset over the flaws in *other* people or things. This inclination toward pickiness has slightly different roots from the first kind of perfectionism.

The picky or overly critical obsessive is practically never content. While most people would prefer an ideal spouse to an imperfect one, they generally accept that much of life is imperfect, and they don't invest too much time or energy in fretting over minor flaws in their mates. If you're a critical obsessive, however, you're a true expert at finding fault with *anything,* and you can't help feeling upset over the shortcomings you find.

With your co-workers you may be diplomatic and supportive, but just as you can always find room for improvement in your own work, it's also a rare piece of others' work that meets with your unqualified acceptance.

Romantic relationships also tend to suffer from this constantly critical attitude. Sarah sadly admitted that her perfectionism had undermined several relationships:

"In each case, I felt more and more upset by the things I saw wrong with each of them," she told me. "The longer I was with each man, the more I felt that his flaws reflected on *me*—my taste, my judgment. I could hardly remember what attracted me to him in the first place. Only later, after he was out of my life, would I see it clearly."

With her ex-husband, Edward, she morosely acknowledged, "I was constantly on his back—criticizing his opinions, his appearance, the way he handled money, his interactions with our son. He finally started to keep things from me just to avoid my disapproval."

Ultimately, Edward grew resentful toward Sarah because he had come to feel so inhibited around her. His resentment then spilled into other aspects of their relationship. He lost interest in their sexual relationship and began spending less time with her. To Sarah this meant she was becoming less attractive to him. She also felt that he was spitefully depriving her of something she wanted, which made her angry. She became even more critical, perpetuating the problem.

Their five-year-old son, Jonathan, also felt belittled by Sarah's pickiness. Her critical nature always seemed to leak through even her best efforts to be supportive. When she praised an art project, or his performance at a Little League game, she couldn't help throwing in a hint as to how he might do better next time. When she watched him interact at a social event, her attention was always seduced by the things he *didn't* do well.

Upon reflection, Sarah could readily recognize the destructive impact of her constant fault-finding, but she felt powerless to change. She'd *always* been picky; to her this trait seemed an immovable pillar of her being, and she even took some pride in it. She saw herself as more discerning than most people. She simply felt condemned to live with its harmful consequences. "My perfectionism has put me through hell," she said. "I feel so lonely. I want so badly to be in a loving relationship with a good man, but I've already ruined a couple of opportunities. I may never get another chance."

If, like Sarah, you constantly focus on the negative, this tendency is likely to sabotage not only your relationships but also your general enjoyment of life. The speck on the glass not only catches your attention but also robs you of the pleasure of drinking from it. When you listen to the stereo, flaws in the sound quality hinder your enjoyment of the music itself. Nor can you abandon yourself to the melody of life. The thing you hear loudest is the static most people ignore. You hear it everywhere, always, and though you may hate it, you don't know how to focus on the more positive elements of life.

Rising Above Perfectionism

The ultimate irony—and tragedy—of perfectionism is that *it simply doesn't work*. It's supposed to earn you rave reviews and exempt you from criticism. Instead it damages both your work and your relationships, and puts you under an unrelenting pressure. If you've concluded that your perfectionism is hurting you, you *can* make changes.

PERFECTLY HUMAN

Part of the Perfectionist's Credo is the notion that other people won't like you as well if you make a mistake, or you don't know things, or you allow your faults to show through. In fact, the opposite is true. Your need to be right all the time often repels friends and associates.

Nobody will ever feel empathy for you, love you, or enjoy being close to you simply because you are right or because you hardly ever make mistakes. It's true that people may admire your abilities or knowledge. Being competent, circumspect, and smart is a plus, but these qualities alone will never win you love.

So try this: next time you are asked a question and don't know the answer, say so. Just say, "I don't know." Don't fudge; don't reel off a dozen possibilities to avoid admitting ignorance; don't offer something you do know but that doesn't answer the question. Just "I don't know." Then keep track of how many friends you lose. See how much less loved you are. Note particularly how much less respect you get.

And the next time you're wrong about something, just admit it. Don't explain why you made the mistake. Don't show how anyone would have made that mistake under the circumstances. Don't insist that your answer actually *was* correct but was misunderstood.

Just confess, "I was wrong about that." Then start counting the people who shrink away from you. I'm exaggerating, of course. But

53

when you start letting your fallibility show, when you let go of your need to know everything and to show how smart you are, you'll feel a burden being lifted. You'll feel more relaxed. It will be easier to smile. You'll be free! And these changes will occur *the very first time* you suppress your perfectionistic need to be infallible.

OVERCOMING THE FEAR OF EMBARRASSMENT

If you find yourself shrinking from certain activities because you dread being embarrassed, ask yourself two questions: Are your social fears and inhibitions preventing you from reaching your full potential or enjoying life? And are you willing to endure a certain amount of anxiety to overcome the problem?

If the answers to both are yes, you stand to gain a lot by systematically exposing yourself to the kinds of situations you fear. Do this little by little if necessary, but start now. For example, if you dread giving oral presentations, start by asking questions as an audience member. Don't wait until you have something brilliant to say. Say anything.

If your anxiety centers on social events such as parties, go to as many as you can, and try to engage in simple conversations: compliment the hostess on her clam dip and ask for the recipe. When you feel at ease doing this, try a longer conversation with someone nonthreatening. The next step would be to chat with a stranger; mentally preparing a list of discussion topics or questions will help.

Follow the same gradual approach in other frightening situations. Take classes that force you to perform in front of others. Join walking groups. Give parties. Tell yourself that it won't be awful if your nervousness shows, or if you make a silly blunder. When these things do happen, and they will, refuse to allow yourself to feel humiliated. Concentrate on the fact that these missteps make you *more* attractive, not less so. You come through as a genuine, vulnerable human being. People can connect with you.

I remember one client, a highly placed engineer in her mid-forties, who confided to me that she had always wanted to be able to dance socially but had never had the courage to do so. She was convinced that she would be mortified if she made mistakes while learning the proper steps. But over time, the more she confronted her fears about what could go wrong, the more they receded. Finally she agreed to take a class in ballroom dancing. The students with whom she studied turned out to be a very supportive, fun-loving group. Although my patient felt shy and tense at first, the group's encouragement quickly helped her to loosen up and participate. Today dancing is no longer a source of envy and fear for her but a source of pleasure, even when she makes mistakes.

CONFRONTING YOUR INNER SABOTEURS

Whether you're writing a paper, painting a living room, or preparing a dinner for guests, if you're a perfectionist you tend to be haunted by such unconscious assumptions as:

- "I couldn't stand it if my work wasn't as good as X's."
- "It's got to be great!"
- "It would be intolerable for them to see me make a mistake."

You may be entirely unaware you're saying such things to yourself; they may sound completely foreign. But from their silent place within, such enduring, submerged beliefs govern many people's more visible behaviors and conscious concerns.

If you're such a person, what you need to know right now is:

- You are *choosing* to think these thoughts.
- They are obliterating your chances at happiness.
- You can start making significant changes right this minute, even with little or no "insight" into your obsessiveness.

For example, let's say you're writing a report or a paper. Maybe you've always thought that a good written report includes every possible angle on the subject, answers every conceivable question, and reflects as much research as is humanly possible.

Well, that's wrong. And it's just that kind of thinking that will prevent you from reaching your creative and productive potential.

In most situations, the best report is the one that's done as well as possible *within the given time limits.*

GETTING YOUR WORK DONE

If getting work done in a timely manner invariably proves to be difficult or painful, you've got to recognize that *your* way (perfection) isn't working. So try this: every time one of those irrational beliefs ("It's got to be done flawlessly!") starts pushing in on you, push back. Tell yourself, "No, it's got to be *completed!*" and keep moving. Focus on how good it feels to make progress on the task. Refuse to judge whether or not you are doing a terrific piece of work. The beauty of finishing on time (or even ahead of schedule) is that you can go back and fine-tune later. Think in terms of movement.

Give serious attention not just to doing the work but scheduling it *realistically.* Perfectionists tend to schedule their time as if they will perform ideally and can anticipate perfect conditions. They assume, for example, that nothing will interrupt them, that fatigue won't hamper their efficiency, that they'll be able to move along at top speed. Instead of blindly making such assumptions, set up realistic checkpoints for achieving certain tasks, even if the work is less than perfect. If you slip behind in one phase, just accept this and get rolling; tighten up a succeeding phase. Accept that your project won't be, *cannot be,* as "perfect" as it could be if you had no deadline and no other responsibilities. Time constraints do shape most things!

Each time you find yourself getting sidetracked by details, or images of how the project will be evaluated, slam your palm down on the desk or your thigh and say "Move!" Take a deep breath, refocus on the goal, and continue on.

Imagine yourself swimming down a river, with the current, toward a goal. You have to arrive there before dark, or it will be too late. Whenever you get sidetracked by details or fine points, envision yourself losing the current and drifting slowly out of the main river into a stream, and from there into a never-ending maze of smaller and smaller streams. They are seductive and interesting, but you lose momentum when you investigate them. Get back into the main river and move into the central current again!

Do the finest piece of work you can, given the limitations of deadlines and the legitimate requirements of your health, family, social life, and leisure pursuits. Remember that all of these dimensions are crucial to your enjoyment of life.

CUTTING THE CLUTTER

Streamline your life, from your verbal style to your physical surroundings. If you know you have a tendency to present too much information verbally, take a step toward correcting that! If you know you'll be in a situation where you'll be tempted to give too many details, prepare in advance by writing down (or at least outlining) what you'd like to cover. Then practice, timing the material as you deliver it. If you run over, edit yourself ruthlessly. Work at it until you can deliver it in *less* than the time allowed. The irrational worries we mentioned earlier will keep trying to assert themselves. They are habits. Don't let them in. Imagine them pulling you away from the current and, just as in completing a task, slap your hand on your desk, say "Move!" take a deep breath, relax, and refocus, then get going.

If it is excess belongings that are cluttering up your life, make the effort to pare them down. Ask yourself how likely you are to need the items you're saving. Review your track record to answer this: How often have you used things you've accumulated? Were those occasions (if any) worth the inconvenience caused by living with the mess? Would it really be so terrible to discard an item you subsequently needed? Are the economics of saving items versus buying replacements really compelling?

Another hidden rationalization for hoarding various items goes like this: you want to do certain things with the items someday (sew that torn dress, read that magazine, repair that car), so you're saving them until you have more time. To get rid of them would be to admit defeat—that you'll *never* do those things you feel you ought to do.

Once again, look at your personal history and ask yourself how likely you are to have a lot more spare time in the foreseeable future. If the answer is "not very likely," then why are you saving these items? Is it to avoid facing the fact that you *can't* do everything that "should" be done—that you're *not* perfect? Wouldn't it be better to face that fact than to continue living with a useless pile of clutter?

AIM FOR AVERAGE

If certain tasks daunt you because you dread having to meet your own standards of perfection, it may help to imagine what a B-minus student, writer, attorney, or radiologist would accomplish. Force yourself to perform only that well, in the interests of accomplishing the task. You'll be amazed not only by the amount of work you'll produce, but also by its quality; it won't suffer as much as you think. You're not a B-minus worker, and that will show through, no matter what you do. And with fewer trivial details to obscure them, your main points will carry more force and be clearer.

You may find it useful to give yourself as many little exercises as you can in being B-minus. Take letter-writing. Instead of watching your unanswered correspondence pile up while you wait for the time and inspiration to produce missives to rival Lord Chesterfield's, give yourself fifteen minutes to produce a brief, very average letter. You'll receive two immediate benefits: you'll have one less letter to write, and your correspondent will be glad to know you're alive and thinking of him or her, however briefly and ineloquently. And again, when you go back and read over your correspondence, you'll be pleasantly surprised by how fluent it is.

In similar fashion, try being a faster, B-minus Christmas shopper, housekeeper, painter, cook, landscaper. And before you insist that you don't want to be a B-minus *anything,* try it a few times. I predict your losses won't even come close to your gains. And the gains will spill over into every aspect of your life. Tasks won't take as long or feel as onerous. And you'll have more free time, while feeling less guilt and pressure. I also predict that when it's truly important to do a good job, you'll do just fine.

OVERCOMING WORK OR STUDY BLOCKS

If perfectionism is inhibiting your progress on certain tasks that require concentration, besides working to change your attitude ("They must be done perfectly!"), you also might try changing the way in which you organize your work time.

Prepare to tackle the troublesome work in short, very structured periods, instead of long, open-ended sessions which create the illusion that you have unlimited time, and thus can dawdle and focus endlessly on details.

Plan a two-hour work session. If you feel you'll need some breaks, schedule them; for example, allow yourself five minutes off between the twenty-fifth and the thirtieth minute of each half hour. Don't spend any of the two-hour period getting ready to work. If you must gather materials or sharpen your pencil, do all that beforehand. Then start the two-hour block exactly at the planned time.

Spend the period in an isolated, silent place; don't work lying down or in a relaxed position. Sitting at a desk or table, keep your feet flat on the floor and have a clock right in front of you. Some people find they work better if they don't have a full stomach; by all means avoid having any alcohol in your system during the work period.

Focus all your attention on the task at hand, trying to move through it at a steady pace, even if you don't resolve every detail. Work as if you were passionately interested in what you're doing, and make an effort to ignore all worries and potential interruptions. If you're trying to read and retain written material, don't underline or outline. These procedures take time away from learning the material and lessen the incentive to master it immediately. If you wish to underline or outline, assign a work period specifically for that, and another for learning the material.

Should your attention wander, stand up but stay right at your workstation and don't sit down until you completely refocus on the material. Don't add any of the standing time onto the end of the block. Regard it simply as lost time that cannot be made up. Don't be surprised if you do a lot of standing the first few sessions.

Stop at precisely the appointed time, even if work remains to be done. Then reward yourself for having completed the time block— with food, pleasure reading, or some other enjoyable activity. If the task is not completed, plan another structured session. You may find that a two-hour block is too long or too short for the particular task you're trying to accomplish. But don't make that decision during a work session; wait a few days to evaluate it.

As you fine-tune this method, you'll find that even though you're spending *less* time working, you'll be much more productive than you ever were when faced with dreaded, interminable sessions. Many of my patients accomplish more in a few two-hour blocks per day than in an unplanned eight-to-nine-hour workday. The quality of their work is every bit as good, and they have far more free time.

CRITIQUING THE CRITIC

What about your tendency to be overly troubled by the flaws and frailties of others, or by their errors? This habit is extremely harmful to your relationships and your mood, but it is also very amenable to change. As with any habit, the key to change lies in increasing your awareness. A habit survives by being sneaky—an automatic part of you that you don't even notice. Don't let it continue being automatic. Turn your pickiness against itself; be as critical as you like of this fault. But don't stop there. Change it!

First, *catch yourself as often as possible thinking judgmental thoughts* about your spouse, child, or employee. Notice how unpleasant the feeling is—the disappointment, resentment, or disgust you are experiencing. Even the momentary self-righteous boost to your own self-esteem is hollow and painful. Acknowledge that your assessment might be accurate: that your child, for instance, really does bite his nails, or have a slight lisp. Then notice that having made the observation is doing you no good whatsoever; that this habit hurts and it has few redeeming qualities compared with the devastation it causes.

Instead of continuing to be upset, use the desk-slap technique (or whatever surface is available, such as your thigh). (If that's too obvious or embarrassing, use another movement, such as blinking once, hard.) Take a deep breath, relax, and immediately shift your attention to a positive aspect of that person or to something good he or she has done. Remember and relive the good feeling toward that person, and simply refuse to return to the critical thoughts.

One thing that perpetuates this bad habit is the fact that you have erroneously come to equate intelligence with your ability to find fault, so the fault-finding is hard to give up. Also, by keeping people on the defensive, you can keep them off the scent of your own shortcomings. Ironically, one of your biggest faults—your pickiness—is painfully obvious to everyone, and it pushes people away.

Keep asking yourself what good your hypercritical nature is doing you versus what it costs. Your child or spouse may be imperfect, but that doesn't mean you have to be upset about it, nor will your being upset change anything. You are making yourself unhappy unnecessarily. If you have a legitimate and constructive gripe, fine. Express it. But don't cripple your relationships out of a need to be preoccupied with what's wrong; with effort, it becomes just as easy to focus on what's *right*.

In the case of Sarah, whose unrelenting pickiness ruined one relationship after another, I pointed out repeatedly in therapy that although she might be *right* about everything she found to criticize, her know-it-all attitude was also costing her. While her ability to see imperfections was helpful in her work as a magazine editor, it was souring many other aspects of her life.

Gradually, Sarah began to be able to catch herself in the act of finding fault. Keeping in mind her awareness of how her pickiness was hurting her, she strove to repress the urge to denigrate the people and things around her, and to steer her thinking toward the good qualities in each. When you do this a few hundred times, new habits develop. They did for Sarah, who came to see that she could enjoy and value something even if it was less than perfect.

Better Than Perfect

Remember, the Perfectionist's Credo that I outlined at the beginning of this chapter is based on inaccurate assumptions. Flawless living is not necessary or possible, or even desirable. You don't have to know everything or perform according to some mythical specifications in order to be worthwhile, loved, or happy.

Who ever taught you otherwise? What genius convinced you that you should never make mistakes? Or that making mistakes proves something is wrong with you? Who made you think that your worth depends on how smart or capable you are? Family? Teachers? Clergy? Who took your wonderful human qualities—your candor and spontaneity, your vulnerability, creativity, and openness—and convinced you that anything else could ever be more valuable or lovable? And who is doing that to you now?

FOUR

Decision and Commitment

You may think you're simply indicating a willingness to go out again, but as far as he's concerned you're endorsing a lifetime commitment that he is quite frankly not ready to make after only one date. . . . From that day forward, if he spots you on the street, he'll spring in the opposite direction to avoid the grave risk that the two of you might meet, which would mean he'd have to ask you if you wanted to get a cup of coffee, and you might say yes, and pretty soon you'd be enjoying each other's company again, and suddenly a clergyman would appear at your table and YOU'D HAVE TO GET MARRIED. AIEEEEEEE.

—DAVE BARRY

Next time you're in a restaurant, glance at some of the people studying their menus at other tables. Most of them are probably enjoying the pleasure of surveying all the choices and knowing they can order what most appeals to them. Others give no more attention to it than they would to tying their shoes; it's a mundane act that they perform without much thought. For some obsessives, however, this simple task can be surprisingly difficult.

Alex, a thirty-seven-year-old pharmaceutical sales rep, one day described for me the turmoil he undergoes routinely in this situation. "I look at the menu and immediately tense up," he said. "I don't know whether I want an omelette, or eggs and bacon, or something different. I could choose pancakes or french toast. Pancakes are a little heavier and probably have more calories, but it's early in the day, so I could eat a bigger meal and burn off the calories later. . . ."

"Suppose you're between an omelette and pancakes," I asked. "What do you say to yourself?"

"If I choose an omelette, then I have to pick what goes into the omelette, right?" He grinned at his own words. "It's just so absurd! There's ham and cheese, but I always get ham and cheese. I think, If I choose this, then I'll miss an opportunity to try something new, something I could add to my repertoire of breakfasts. But on the other hand, it might not be good. And then I will have wasted a choice. I'll feel angry. I'll feel like I got ripped off by my own choice. I will have made a mistake."

Deciding on breakfast was the least of Alex's problems with decision-making and commitment. He had turned to therapy because he was in agony over his four-year-long relationship with Cicely. Although he loved her and felt some pressure to have children while it was still possible, Alex was bothered by what he saw as certain shortcomings in Cicely's personality, various things that he conceded seemed minor, but that he feared might haunt him if they got married. At times his preoccupation with those issues brought him to the verge of breaking up with her, but then the thought of all the happiness they had enjoyed over the years would flood over him, and he'd be filled with grief at the thought of losing her forever. He desperately yearned to "get his life moving," with Cicely or without her, and he inwardly despised his own indecisiveness, yet he continued to feel paralyzed.

One time I asked Alex to pay attention to all the occasions on which decision-making caused him problems in the course of a week, and he came back with a list including everything from selecting a shirt in the morning to buying a condominium. "I even obsess over picking out a shampoo!" he exclaimed, again laughing. "They don't make my usual brand anymore. I spent ten minutes at the drugstore trying to decide what to buy. When I walked out of there, I was saying, 'Alex, here you go again! Why don't you just pick one of each and throw away the ones you don't like? You can afford it.' But I don't *want* to throw one away. I'm obsessed with making the right decision beforehand and not having to deal with making a mistake."

The Risk of Error

Alex, as you can plainly see, harbors the Perfectionist's Credo: *I can and must avoid making any mistakes.* Decisions and commitments often are the perfectionist's nemeses because each decision or commitment carries the risk of being wrong. To perfectionists, being wrong isn't something negligible. It's a threat to the very essence of their self-image, which depends partly on keeping the Credo intact.

That's not to say that all obsessives—even very perfectionistic ones—react the same way to *all* decisions and commitments. Human behavior can't be reduced to formulas. In fact, a person may find it impossible to make a decision Wednesday that he made with ease on Monday.

Some individuals have trouble only with certain *types* of decisions. Alex, for example, reports that he rarely has trouble making decisions related to his work. Doug, a high school vice-principal, easily made the decision to get married and felt comfortably committed to his wife. But he was having a terrible time deciding whether or not to start a family.

"Everything costs so much; I worry about being able to provide for any children. I'm also older now [in his late thirties], and I wonder if I have the energy—emotional and physical—that it takes to be a good parent. On the other hand, I've always enjoyed kids, and I get along really well with them. At times I love the thought of having my own. Then I think of everything I'd have to give up, both in terms of time and material luxuries. But I have plenty of friends with children who attest eloquently to the compensations.

"Moira [his wife] seems to be leaning more and more toward having children, and that only increases the pressure I feel. I realize that if we wait too long, we may not be able to have any even if we want them, and that would be horrible! But it would also be wrong to have children and wind up resenting them."

Gina reported having the most trouble deciding how her family should spend its vacations.

"I feel I have to plan this time in the best possible way. Each time we sketch out a possibility, all the but-ifs and what-ifs come out. For example, I really wanted to drive up the coast over the holidays, but I couldn't decide exactly when to leave; I thought maybe we'd feel too rushed if we left the day after Christmas. Then I spent weeks getting guidebooks and researching hotels; by the time I decided where I wanted to stay, I couldn't get reservations, and I worried that if we just took off without them, we'd be stranded. This has happened before; I can't make a decision in time and I wind up doing *nothing*, which is worse than any of the potential problems that held me back."

Avoiding Decisions

Such waffling is typical of the behavior of many obsessives faced with a decision. They see all the pros and cons of any choice, all the while hoping that enough facts will pile up on one side to tip the balance and spare them the responsibility for deciding. They weigh and think, think and weigh.

Just as they start to lean one way, they notice an unreckoned drawback. Then an overlooked option appears and pulls them toward *that* direction. But they soon discover a new shortcoming of that plan and start back toward the original scheme.

After agonizing for a while, they may resort to an "objective" method, such as making exhaustive lists of the pros and cons. If it's a draw, they may weight each item according to importance, and even apply a complex tie-breaking formula—anything to avoid having to take personal responsibility for the outcome. Alas, the balance never seems to tip, and their torment continues.

LIVING IN ONE'S HEAD

Postponing decision-making until they get enough facts to guarantee the "right" choice is another way obsessives avoid action and its attendant risk of error. I think of Annette, a hardworking young newspaper ad saleswoman. When she realized she needed to buy a new car, she spent months gathering brochures, test-driving possible alternatives, reading *Consumer Reports,* getting advice from friends, and contrasting features and prices. She contended that all of this activity was simply reasonable preparation for an intelligent decision, and of course there is truth to this position. But Annette remained unaware of the greater truth: that her main goal was to avoid error, even at the cost of making no decision at all.

She finally narrowed her options to a few final items—the financing terms, the color, the model—but she somehow couldn't choose. Each answer evoked a new set of doubts. One dealer was closer to her home but didn't have the car in blue. One had it in blue but was charging more. To an outsider, it was clear that any of the alternatives could be lived with, but Annette stubbornly resisted this conclusion.

Instead she was comfortable only as long as all the action was as preparation. In car-buying as in many areas of her life, *actual movement* frightens Annette because action always carries with it the danger of error. No sooner is she ready to make a move than she starts doubting and stalling for more time. Doggedly she resists seeing that her indecisiveness is actually an unconscious decision *not* to choose. Her hidden agenda is to avoid the risk of being wrong and contradicting the Credo.

This goal differs markedly from that held by people who typically make decisions in a healthier, less painful manner. Such people accept that their decisions will be strongly influenced by their likes and dislikes, hunches, and yearnings. They may well seek some facts to supplement this subjective starting ground, but their goal throughout the process is to act, as quickly and as reasonably as possible, and they accept implicitly that there is no way to do so in a fail-safe manner. Furthermore, they trust that they usually *won't* make awful blunders. They know that they occasionally risk mistakes, regrets, and dangers, but they also accept that risk is part of life. So they decide and move on. They're more involved with *living* than with evaluating themselves.

For obsessives like Annette, in contrast, action is the enemy. The status quo is an overly protective friend. Consciously this sort of person honestly thinks she wants to take action. In fact, she will often complain, "I just *hate* this indecisiveness." But another part of her wants to live mainly in her fantasy. This part wants to postpone, forever, testing the Perfectionist's Credo by deciding and acting.

Of course, life demands movement. In the case of Annette's search for a new car, outside circumstances finally forced her hand when her old car broke down and she faced exorbitant repair bills. By that time, no dealers happened to have Annette's first choice, so she wound up buying a model that was lower down on her list.

ESCAPE HATCHES

Oddly enough, this didn't seem to bother her too much. In fact, it gave her a wonderful excuse should the car turn out to have been a poor choice; she could always tell herself, "I had to take what I could get; it's not as if I actually *chose* this one."

This is only one of many escape hatches that allow decision-fearing obsessives to make decisions without challenging the Perfectionist's Credo. Sometimes such people will strive to make it look—to themselves as well as others—as if they're not *really* deciding but instead are merely yielding to the weight of evidence. When Alex is in a restaurant agonizing over whether to order the scampi or the linguini, he yearns for the waiter to say that customers have been very pleased with one and disappointed with the other. It doesn't have to be true. As long as the balance has been tipped by an outside event, it is no longer Alex's own decision, and the Credo is spared a challenge.

Yet another way of making a decision look like a non-decision is to cling to doubts, reservations, and qualifications even as you decide. You say, for instance, "I'll take this jacket only because it doesn't need alterations and I need to wear it tonight. It might not be the best choice, but what can you expect under the circumstances?" If the choice doesn't work out, it was only a half-decision in the first place. Since you didn't give it your best effort, you remain potentially infallible.

Avoiding Commitment

The Perfectionist's Credo can cause problems with more than decision-making. As was the case with Alex, it also can wreak havoc with one's ability to make commitments.

Commitment is the final phase of decision-making. It's the act of pledging oneself to someone or something and giving up other options. Once a decision is experienced as irreversible or unchangeable, it becomes a commitment. For example, you may *decide* to buy the brown shoes instead of the black ones. But you haven't really made a *commitment* to your choice until you're at the cash register—and even then it's not irreversible. Once you've paid for the shoes, the commitment becomes stronger, but only when you take them home and wear them does the commitment become complete. You have closed off all options and can no longer change directions; you are totally committed. You can see why many obsessives would fear commitment. Anyone who is afraid of making a wrong decision or choice would be doubly threatened if he or she saw that decision or choice as irrevocable.

TENTATIVENESS

Just as some obsessives fall back on various escape hatches to diminish the threat of decision-making, some will try to forestall commitment through *tentativeness.* Even as they lean toward action, they try to keep one foot on the path they decided not to take. Forced to remove that foot, they may feel optionless and become nervous.

I've known people who have bought major furnishings, taken them home, and then stubbornly resisted removing the plastic covering for months as they vacillated over the possibility of taking the item back and exchanging it for something else. They fend off their commitment fears by postponing closure.

Another good example of tentativeness can be found in the way many obsessives express themselves. In offering personal opinions, they try to keep their options open by qualifying practically everything they say. Their speech is loaded with such qualifiers as "I guess," "I think," and "I'm not sure, but it seems to me that maybe . . ."

When you ask such a person for a recommendation, you get a

rundown on every consideration instead of a single straightforward opinion. "Well, you might enjoy [a given play] if you like contemporary drama," he may say. "It's provocative, but you might find it a bit grim. Another possiblity is X, where the production is quite stunning. The tickets are the most expensive in town, however, and you might also consider Z."

Forced to take a position or make a prediction, this type of person will do so only with reservations. He will say, "The Chargers should win tomorrow's game, but since they're playing in Denver and So-and-so's knee is sore, it wouldn't surprise me if they lost." He points out that he has mixed feelings about the political candidate or restaurant under discussion, and that he can see both sides of the issue. He leaves himself room to shift, and so avoids ever being just plain wrong, which would clash with his need to be perfect. Qualifiers enable him to keep the exit doors open.

I hardly need to point out the effect of this kind of tentativeness on others. Friends and colleagues get frustrated when they can't tell what you really feel or think. Your vagueness makes it hard to know you and feel connected to you. And if you consistently pull back from clearly airing your opinions, you suffer in other ways too. You never get to taste the pleasure of unmuddied self-expression, and you lose the opportunity to see your opinions tested and challenged. In fact, you may not even know what they are!

Fear of Romantic Commitments

Commitment-fearing obsessives suffer most in the romantic realm. It's not that they can't fall in love. On the contrary, I've known obsessives who are addicted to the high-adrenaline excitement of romance in its early phases, and who fall in love time after time. They may even be capable of balancing comfortably in a love relationship for long periods of time. But whenever they sense an ultimatum to *commit* themselves in some way to a long-term, exclusive relationship with their romantic partner, their anxiety soars. They are torn. If they get up and walk away, they will still have their freedom, but will have lost a precious source of intimacy and joy. More important, they may have made an irreversible error that will haunt them forever. Perhaps they will never fall in love again. Or, if they do, maybe no subsequent partner will ever measure up to the lost love.

On the other hand, the thought of getting married feels like entering a tunnel that leads directly from the moment of commitment to the grave. "I feel like a part of me would be dying," groaned Marty, a thirty-nine-year-old mechanical engineer, in describing how he felt about acceding to his girlfriend Janet's wishes for marriage and a family. "In order to have her, I have to give up my freedom; I have to give up the option of other women. And I'm afraid to do that. The bottom line is I feel like I'm going to miss out. I don't want to give up anything because I'm afraid it will be a mistake and I'll regret it. A lot of my happiness in life has come from the initial stages of a relationship—getting close to someone and falling in love with her."

Marty had never had any trouble doing this. In fact, he had dated many attractive, desirable women. But eventually he became bored and then oppressed by each one, especially when she showed any sign of hoping for a commitment. "All my relationships have ended up the same way," he told me, "with painful feelings."

As the years passed, he gradually began to see his hopes of finding the perfect wife and having children fade. Then he began dating Janet, a talented and vivacious realtor with an excellent sense of humor. Although Marty couldn't detect *any* serious flaws in her, each time he considered making a permanent commitment to her, he was plunged into another agony of indecision. "I feel like if I make that decision

I'll be trapped forever. I'm afraid I'll make the commitment one day and the next day I'll think it was a mistake. At the same time, I hate myself for being so wishy-washy. I don't want to be this way."

Janet expressed her frustration by informing Marty she was going off on a vacation by herself; he was crushed, and terrified that she would meet someone else. Eventually, Marty proposed marriage and Janet relented. Almost immediately, however, he found himself stalling at her requests for an engagement ring; nor could he bring himself to announce the engagement to friends and family.

Janet put up with this for a few more weeks, then *she* called off the engagement and stuck by her refusal to see him anymore, despite his begging for another chance. After about six weeks of profound depression, Marty finally resigned himself to losing her and began dating another woman. Yet in some part of his consciousness he continued to feel as if he still had the option of getting Janet back. This became clear more than a year after he broke up with her, when he received an invitation to her upcoming wedding, and his depression recurred.

This cycle of ultimatum-withdrawal-rapprochement is a common one among commitment-fearing obsessives. When the ultimatum looms, such people may lose interest in the relationship, either gradually or with shocking suddenness. The terror of commitment also may trigger symptoms such as anxiety, palpitations, insomnia, or various gastrointestinal upsets. The obsessive then may withdraw from the relationship emotionally or physically, or he may start behaving in ways that provoke the other person to get out of it—thus enabling the obsessive to escape blame-free. But many times when the commitment-seeking partner finally does walk away, the obsessive—now terrified that an end to the relationship may be an irreversible mistake—will try to win the partner back. The relationship may return to a state of equilibrium again—until another ultimatum surfaces. And then the cycle continues.

WHO'S AFRAID OF ROMANTIC COMMITMENTS?

Although the majority of my patients who fear romantic commitments have been obsessive men like Marty, I have also known women to be the phobic party in these matches. Sometimes both partners share the same hidden terror of commitment.

In the case of Denise, that terror remained submerged for years. A vibrant and beautiful physical therapist, Denise first came to see me for depression over her inability to sustain a lasting relationship. She had gotten involved with one man after another who had set limits on their relationship and either resisted or fled whenever Denise had sought to expand those limits.

Soon after we met, she listed what she thought were the possible causes of her problem: she was a bad judge of men; she was "doing something" that prevented her lovers from wanting a committed, long-term relationship with her; good men were simply impossible to find. After each breakup she was crushed, thinking that perhaps she had some basic flaw that inevitably would appear as soon as a man got close. Each time she wept for weeks, convinced that it was her fate to be alone forever. Exacerbating her feelings of despair was the fact that throughout her childhood the males in her family had belittled her, making her doubt that she was lovable or attractive.

Denise's many personal strengths made it clear there was more to her problem than just bad luck. Then she met Kenny, a warm, engaging man her own age who conspicuously failed to erect the sort of psychic barriers put up by Denise's previous lovers. Kenny, in fact, eventually began pressing her to spend one weeknight with him, in addition to the pattern into which they had settled of one night per weekend. And to her own amazement, Denise reacted with a mixture of intense anxiety and resistance! Even though she really liked Kenny, she made excuses for *not* spending more time with him. "I don't want to cut out any of my jogging time," she told me. "And I'm also afraid to cut back on the little time I devote to practicing the guitar. And what if he insists that I get rid of my cats?" I suggested that maybe Denise's reaction indicated that she herself had serious fears of making a commitment to any man, and that perhaps these fears had contributed to her string of romantic disasters. After some soul-searching, she agreed, and eventually was able to begin to change her behavior.

THE UNCOMMITTED MARRIAGE

Some individuals may actually go through the motions of making a commitment, moving in with their partner, even getting married. But years later their behavior and their attitude may continue to reflect a desperate desire to keep their options open.

Bart, an architect, declared at our first meeting, "In a nutshell, my problem is women." For five years he had been married to a woman named Bea, and had gradually lost interest in her, physically and emotionally, over the course of their marriage. When I met him, he was plagued by sexual fantasies of other women and had had three short-lived extramarital affairs.

Bart went so far as to tell Bea that he wanted to see other women, and when she objected to this, he became angry. However, when Bea began to voice her own doubts about the future of their marriage, *Bart* felt surprisingly anxious. He told me, "It's one of the worst possible things that could happen. I see divorce as one of the ultimate expressions of failure."

Not long afterward, Bart declared that he could no longer tolerate being torn between preserving his marriage and getting involved with other attractive women. He decided to concentrate on improving his marriage, and I suggested a brief trial of total commitment, meaning a refusal to entertain his doubts or think longingly of other women, and a wholehearted attempt to do everything in his power to enjoy the many positive aspects of his marriage. Bart agreed to try, but at our next meeting he reported, "Last week I left here in a state of panic about this whole commitment thing. What you said made good sense, but to make that much of a commitment, even for just a few weeks, feels impossible."

He realized that whenever he was with Bea he typically focused on his conflict over their marriage, or dwelt on her flaws:

"In my usual state, I pretend to be happy, but really feel anxiety or anger that I don't express. . . . Bea asks, 'Why don't you let yourself be happy?' But that ties in with commitment. When we're together and I'm feeling happy, it's as if I'm conceding that I'm going to be married to Bea forever, and that really depresses me."

Armed with this new self-awareness, he began working on small but specific adjustments in his attitude. One Sunday afternoon, for instance, he concentrated on relaxing and allowing himself to enjoy some time with Bea, shutting his mind to his doubts. He was pleasantly surprised when his positive feelings toward her persisted into the week—longer than they had in years.

Over time, Bart's resolve to stay in the marriage grew stronger. As he accumulated positive experiences with Bea and allowed himself to "register" them, he was slowly able to relinquish much of his need to keep his options open for other relationships. He felt a lot of sadness as he did this; like many people, he experienced a form of genuine grief as he watched his fantasies die. But Bart continued to work on his marriage after ending therapy with me, and several years later he appeared to have succeeded at making his peace with it.

Overcoming Indecisiveness and the Fear of Commitment

If a person cannot make decisions or avoids commitments because he wants to "hold on to his options," he had better be enjoying them. They are expensive. Consider some of the costs:

- You suffer every time you can't decide about something or face a potential commitment. It is grueling and excruciating to be torn apart this way.

- Hundreds, even thousands, of hours of your life are wasted on trying to make up your mind or ruminating over decisions already made. Imagine how much energy all this effort costs. And for what? Does all the waffling and stalling make the decisions turn out that much better?

- Indecisiveness and fear of commitment are sure to cause you to miss numerous opportunities, from financial ventures to long-term romantic relationships. There's a lot of truth to the old adage: Not to decide *is* to decide, and often for the worse.

- A tentative attitude prevents you from giving anything your best effort. To realize the full extent of your capacities—to maximize your creativity, talents, and ability to experience life—you must sometimes put aside doubts. This is the only way to have all of yourself available for a total effort at anything.

If you have trouble with decision-making, your life may move along after a fashion; you do manage to get into or out of jobs, relationships, projects, purchases. But you rarely do these things directly and cleanly,

cating, and once the decision is made, rather than second-guessing it, they focus on making the most of it. Because they are able to enjoy the positive aspects of the path chosen, their minds usually associate the act of deciding with pleasure, not pain. This association perpetuates a willingness to keep making choices rather than shy away from them.

Making Decisions— A Commonsense Approach

To overcome a difficulty with decision-making and commitments, start to observe the problem *as it is happening* and label it: "This is a chronic problem for me." Don't let it be automatic anymore.

Pay attention to any anxiety you feel when someone pushes you for a direct, unequivocal answer, or asks you to commit yourself to a specific option. Notice your apprehension when it's time to finalize a major purchase, or close a deal. Stop and search for the cause of your anxiety. Dig for the specific fears.

Here are some common examples:

- It would be awful to overlook some flaw in this car, and then buy it, only to see the flaw surface later.
- If I wait long enough, facts will accumulate and I'll be assured of making the "right" decision.
- I couldn't bear it if anyone saw that I made a wrong choice.
- If I make this date, I might not feel like going when the time comes, and then I'll regret the decision. And good people don't cancel or change their minds, so once I make the date, I'm really trapped.
- Once I make this purchase, I'm stuck with it forever.
- My life would be ruined if I got engaged—or worse, married!—and later had some regrets.

- It would be terrible to have committed myself to an appointment if something preferable came along later for the same time.
- I can't take a stand because I'm not sure I'll feel the same way later, and changing my mind would make me look like a fool.

Once you've uncovered the particular thoughts that plague you, think about them one by one. For the most part, they are either inaccurate statements, exaggerations, or arbitrary assumptions badly in need of revision. And they are damaging you terribly. You may have hosted such beliefs for a long time, but that doesn't make them true, and you need not hold on to them. Starting right now, you can challenge these counterproductive ideas and replace them with sound reasoning.

How true is it, for instance, that you're stuck with that shirt or even that car "forever"? And even if you did have to keep it for a while, would that necessarily be "awful"? Chances are, the only thing that makes it awful, rather than just inconvenient or uncomfortable, is *your labeling it* as such and then stubbornly dwelling upon that idea.

How unbearable is it to miss out on a better way to spend an evening because you closed your options too early?

Are you really a bad person if you change your mind when conditions change or when unexpected contingencies arise? Are you sure that the other person would stop liking you? And if that did happen, is it true you couldn't live with it?

Are all commitments truly irreversible?

Concentrate on how extreme this thinking is. Don't ever tell yourself, "I couldn't stand it if such and such happened," unless you're sure that's true. (I would wager that nine times out of ten, it isn't.) I am stressing this because it's crucial to your happiness that you learn to distinguish between temporary discomfort and something intolerable.

So take the time to think about it now and every time the opportunity arises. Don't let old, untested, irrational thinking habits continue to dictate what you are going to feel. *Think as a person who truly wants to be happier, someone who will do everything possible to make his or her life better.*

ON TO ACTION

After pinpointing and critiquing the inaccurate assumptions that impede your decision-making, resolve to act. When a decision must be made, allow yourself a reasonable period to consider the available facts (as well as your own likes and dislikes), then register the direction in which you are leaning. Acknowledge that it has its drawbacks, as every option does, and that it's not fail-safe; no decision is. Grant that it might turn out to be wrong. And just this once, fight the false notion that there is always a single correct choice and that it's always knowable in advance. Accept that you *can* live with something less than perfection. Don't get stuck in that paralyzing cycle of doubts and reservations. You've probably already been through them ad nauseam.

Once you've made the decision, refuse to question your choice. Tell yourself that you can continue to doubt other choices if you must, but *in this one case*, you're not going to allow yourself to wonder about the path not taken. And refuse to judge yourself. Hold on to the knowledge that your decision, good or bad, says absolutely nothing about your worth or competence as a person. Concentrate on enjoying the direction you have chosen, rather than the one you did not.

Once you've tried this, you should be able to use the memory of the experience to repeat your success (success in the sense of your refusal to inflict unnecessary pain on yourself). Call up the sense of accomplishment that you felt, of painless forward motion, and use those good feelings as incentives to make other decisions.

At times you may still find yourself second-guessing your decisions, especially when you are tired or in a bad mood. (This is when old habits tend to reappear.) Try to catch yourself, and acknowledge that, even though it's automatic, it's something you are actively choosing to do, and you can choose otherwise.

Tell yourself that you refuse to continue inflicting such pain upon yourself. Then take a deep breath, let go of the conflicted thoughts, and get on with whatever you were doing.

I'm not suggesting you should never doubt, change your mind, or reverse your course. If it becomes obvious that your path is wrong and another would clearly be better, by all means change directions. Then do everything in your power to make *that* decision work. Enjoy the positive aspects of the new direction, and resist dwelling on doubts about it.

Making Romantic Commitments

This same approach can help reduce the pain and anxiety of making romantic commitments. Next time you're torn by an ultimatum either to make a commitment or end an important relationship, clarify the thoughts that are causing your anxiety. You'll probably find two sets of concerns locked in battle within you.

If I don't commit:

- I will feel guilty about dashing X's hopes after all this time.
- I might discover later that I want him or her back.
- I might never again meet someone who could love me as much.
- His/her leaving will make me unbearably sad.

But if I do make the commitment:

- I might wind up regretting that I chose X and be trapped by my conscience in a bad relationship.

- I'll be accepting the intolerable certainty of never falling in love again.
- Someone with whom I could have a better relationship might come along, and I would be tied up.
- I'll be giving up my freedom, and just *thinking* about that feels horrible, almost like dying.

Now consider these more reasonable beliefs:

- Although it's sad and painful to end a love relationship, you would recover from such a loss (as would your loved one). The pain would be neither intolerable nor endless, even though it might *seem* that way for a time. And you would almost certainly be able to find another relationship eventually.

- On the other hand, if you did make the commitment, it wouldn't be irreversible. No commitment to a relationship ever is. Though you shouldn't ever enter a relationship with the idea of bailing out when it gets difficult, if it becomes clear that it won't work, even after every effort to resolve the problems, you can end it. It would be difficult, but you could if you had to.

- If you're so close to committing to X, how unsuitable a choice could he or she be? X might well have some flaws, like most human beings, and it's true that a better choice for you might someday appear, but don't use these arguments to disguise an exaggerated fear of commitment. If the main obstacle is your terror of closing options, the same problem is bound to come up in future relationships, no matter who your partner is.

- Finally, it's true that giving up the fantasy of ever having a new love is a painful loss, but it's not unbearable unless you decide it is. If you insist on telling yourself you can't stand the thought of giving that up, fine. Have it your way. But you don't have to think that. Giving up some degree of freedom is in fact a painful thing for most people, but it's a necessary part of attaining some of the things you want. Losing your freedom may *feel* like a form of dying, but again, that's only so because you have decided to see it that way. Try to concentrate instead on how much you are gaining.

This systematic approach helped Belle, a thirty-year-old dietitian who had gone through an extended period without any romantic relationships, and was beginning to fear that she might always be alone. When she met Clifford, happiness and an initial sense of relief washed over her. Bright, funny, and successful, Clifford obviously loved her and the two consistently got along well. But after a year Belle began to focus upon Clifford's tendency to be self-centered and plagued by worries.

By the time we met, Belle was telling herself daily that the relationship was unsatisfactory and she should get out before Clifford could accuse her of leading him on. On the other hand, she remembered how frightened and anxious she had been when alone. She waffled back and forth, back and forth.

"I'm sure I'll always regret it if I don't get out," she told me. "I'll always wonder if I might have found somebody I would get along with better. It really bothers me that I'm not any closer to a decision. I know it's unfair to Clifford. He has no idea how I feel. I think that for me to get out, he'll have to ask me to live with him, and I won't be able to do it."

Sure enough, Clifford did soon ask her to move in, and Belle's anxiety level shot sky-high. But after more agonizing, she decided she *would* try moving in with him. And not long afterward, she agreed that since she wasn't making any moves to get out of the relationship, she would try to make the most of it.

Whenever Belle began to list Clifford's faults and derelictions, I would ask her what good this line of thought was accomplishing. Eventually she worked on catching herself at recycling doubts. We talked about how her chronic fault-finding and second-guessing were not leading to any action. She was entertaining them to continue the *illusion* of options so that she could feel less trapped in the relationship. But all this focusing on imperfections was harming the relationship.

She eventually realized that, deep down, fear was preventing her from letting her objections go, lest she become so close and so connected to Clifford that she might *never* be able to get out, a prospect that terrified her. Eventually, though, she felt confident enough to discard the illusion of a safety net. She and Clifford married, and appeared to be doing well some years later.

Your Choice

I'm not making a blanket recommendation that you commit to your current romance, job, or anything else; I don't have to live with the results. *You alone* must decide how much of your reluctance is legitimate and how much is your fear of commitment.

If it's only reasonable caution, you'll resolve your doubts as new data come in. But if the main obstacle is a fear of decisions and commitments, data won't help. In fact, you will just use this additional information to justify your paralysis. You'll waver, anguished, until external matters decide for you or until you can't stand vacillating anymore and jump in or out on impulse.

The most important thing to remember is how much depends on your perceptions. You can choose to see commitment as an unbearable risk, and the end of your freedom. Or you can choose to see it as the only way to stop this chronic feeling of painful isolation and lost time.

FIVE

Demand-Sensitivity and Demand-Resistance

Mary, Mary, quite contrary,
How does your garden grow?
—NURSERY RHYME

C arla, a thirty-two-year-old teacher, tried to explain her reluctance to make love to Bernie, her husband of four years:

"I don't know what the problem is, but I rarely seem to want to have sex with him anymore. The thing is, when we do have sex I usually enjoy it, and I find Bernie physically attractive. I sometimes have erotic thoughts about him when I'm at work or when we're out to dinner with friends. And we really do love each other. But for some reason I find myself procrastinating about coming to bed, waiting until he's likely to be asleep. I'm worried that if our love life deteriorates any further, he may start to think about other women. Yet even though I *want* our sex life to improve, when we have an opportunity to make love, I seem to lose interest."

Jason's job as a political consultant requires him to produce a steady stream of written analyses. Yet, with increasing regularity, he finds one thing after another interfering with his ability to work. He also has difficulty starting household projects, even enjoyable ones. And because he has trouble getting himself into bed at a reasonable hour, he's chronically tired and lethargic. One day in my office when he was particularly exhausted, he told me he had stayed up late the night before, zapping from one "dumb" television program to another.

"If the shows were 'dumb,' why did you keep watching?" I asked.

"I guess I felt too tired to work, but I didn't want to go to bed."

"Why not?"

"I don't know. In fact, I'd intended to go to bed. I had said to myself, 'You've got to go to bed early tonight.' "

"Got to?"

"It sounds as if I'm giving myself orders," he said, grinning.

"So what prevented you from going to bed?"

"I don't know!"

Gordon came to me for help with his persistent insomnia, stomach disorders, and feelings of anxiety. It quickly became apparent that he exhibited a number of classic obsessive traits, so I wasn't surprised to hear his wife, Lorraine, relate the following: "I've learned not to come out and say it when I want Gordon to do something. If I *don't* ask, he'll do it, but if I say something, I never know when I'll see some action. I recently made the mistake of asking him to fill out his part of a credit application. He said he would, and I know he wants the charge card, but that was three weeks ago. The paperwork has been posted on the refrigerator ever since. He still says he's going to get to it, but somehow the right moment never seems to arise."

What's going on here? What's preventing these people from doing things that each of them seemingly *wants* to do?

Many different factors *could* explain their behavior. But in these particular cases, the two powerful factors were *a special sensitivity to perceived demands or expectations, and a negative inner response to these demands.*

I call these two conditions "demand-sensitivity" and "demand-resistance." Although they don't always occur simultaneously, they are related, and both frequently affect the obsessive person.

Demand-Sensitivity

Obsessives tend to be especially sensitive to demands, either real or imagined, that are placed upon them. One aspect of demand-sensitivity is the tendency to "hear" demands or expectations in an exaggerated way. When the boss says he'd like to have something on his desk by Wednesday, the obsessive person often feels the expectation more acutely than others. In fact he often hears more of an imperative than the boss intended.

The obsessive person also exaggerates more subtle or inferred demands. Suppose, for instance, I've drafted a letter to the editor of the local newspaper and have given it to you, saying, "If you have a chance, let me know what you think of it." If you're a demand-sensitive obsessive, you'll feel a pressure not only to look over the piece, but to offer helpful suggestions and return the material to me as soon as possible. While you may not actually *do* these things, you'll probably perceive my request as much more of a demand than it was, and even resent me for placing such a burden on you!

PHANTOM OBLIGATIONS

Everyday living presents thousands of situations in which we are expected to conform to certain unstated expectations or conventions. For instance:

- In most cultures, men are expected to make the first move in dating.
- We are supposed to show deference to our elders, or to our superiors at work.
- Marriage carries with it a tacit imperative to have sex with or show affection to one's spouse.
- We are supposed to be polite.

Whether or not the obsessive person complies with them, he is exquisitely attuned to these and other unstated obligations. In fact he hears them as if they were shouted through a bullhorn. Placed in a new situation, his first concern often is getting the lay of the land, discovering what the rules are. Within my therapy groups, for example, it's usually one of the obsessive patients who will ask whether the group "should" be talking about a particular subject. Send him on a luxury cruise, and he'll worry about how much he's "supposed" to tip the maid and the stewards.

WANTS BECOME SHOULDS

In similar fashion, obsessive people will read demands or expectations into situations, whether or not such demands really exist. During one of our meetings, a perfectionistic photographer named Liz happened to mention a brief list of things she wanted to do in the upcoming week. Although I had neither asked her to make the list nor suggested she do the things on it, the following week she sheepishly confessed, "I didn't do all the things I was supposed to do this past week, so I don't feel I have much to talk about." She spoke as though *I* had expected her to accomplish the things on the list and as though she had to answer to *me*, even though I had nothing to do with the plan.

Between the moment when she first conceived of the list and our next meeting, an important change took place in Liz's thinking. At some point—probably almost immediately after she made the list—her perception became distorted. Instead of seeing the listed activities as things she *wanted* to do, she began to view them as tasks imposed upon her, which she had some sort of moral obligation to fulfill.

I see this transformation over and over in my obsessive patients. Somehow, "I want" turns into "I should." In fact, the phrase "I want" is a rarity in their thinking and their vocabulary. Instead of "I *want* to," they usually experience and say, "I *ought* to," "I *must,*" or "I *should.*" Volition is replaced by obligation. And similarly, rather than saying, "I don't want to," they say, "I can't."

The unconscious conversion of "I want" into "I should" is a childhood safety-seeking maneuver that becomes ingrained in the obsessive's character, a maneuver that comes to serve many motives. For example, people who need to be above reproach are often most comfortable when they feel their decisions and actions are being dictated by outside forces. It's harder to criticize someone who's "only following orders," as opposed to one doing something he initiated himself. Also, thinking and speaking in such terms as "I should" or "I have to" feels and sounds less selfish and somehow more moral and responsible than "I want" or "I'd like." In the obsessive's worldview, where conscientiousness is king, it's better to be fulfilling one's duty than satisfying one's own needs.

THE PRICE OF DEMAND-SENSITIVITY

But the costs of unconsciously disowning one's desires are high. A special joy and fulfillment spring from realizing goals that have been freely chosen. In contrast, when most of your activities feel like obligations, you can reach a point where *nothing* gives you pleasure, and life feels meaningless. You don't feel like an active participant, taking what enjoyment you can in life, but instead experience yourself as a passive recipient, grinding away at the obligations that are laid upon you. You may feel powerless, as if you lack control over your life—a very uncomfortable state.

Indeed, you may lack a clear, stable sense of self—of who you are. You may know what you do well, what you've achieved, whom you dislike, what frightens you. These sorts of things do *contribute* to our sense of identity, but they aren't enough. A solid sense of self requires a consistent awareness of your volitional side—what you *want.* Without that anchor, you wind up feeling insubstantial and passive, and you may feel more vulnerable to external influences, especially the wishes of others. Because you feel (at an unconscious level) as if your sense of self—unanchored as it is—can at any moment be overrun by more powerful outside forces, you are compelled to guard against people who seem strong or intrusive, or who get too close.

Demand-Resistance

For many of my patients, this sense of vulnerability appears to have begun early in childhood. One patient, a thirty-year-old computer programmer named Gerald, could remember and describe explicitly the sensation of feeling overwhelmed by his mother at a very young age. Gerald saw a clear connection between his oppositional adult self and the child who so often had felt threatened by his mother's demands.

"One major source of confrontation was food. Even when I was hungry, I resented how my mother controlled my meals. She gave me more than I wanted; she made me eat foods she knew I didn't like without giving me the chance to say 'No!' It was like I was an extension of *her* needs, as if she were saying, 'If *you* eat, *I'll* be happy.' I was just mirroring something in her. I felt that if I just automatically complied with whatever she asked, I'd be asked to do it again. And I'd be asked to do so many things, I'd always be *reacting* and never stopping to know what *I* wanted."

"And what then?"

"I wouldn't *be* there. I wouldn't exist! There would be no 'I'!"

Eventually, Gerald found a weapon. "The weapon was holding back," he told me. "If I didn't eat, it drove my mother crazy. If I withheld affection, it caused my parents pain. It made me feel powerful, in control."

Gerald recalled noting how pleased his parents were at his junior high school graduation. "From that time on, I held back with my performance. And I think I'm still doing it. When I know somebody wants something from me, I don't do it. It's so automatic, it ends up being more important for me to hold back than to decide what I want."

I would describe Gerald as intensely "demand-resistant"—that is, inclined to balk at various expectations *simply because they are perceived as demands.* As Gerald discovered, demand-resistance is closely connected with interpersonal control. First, it's a way of safeguarding one's fragile sense of self by refusing to be overpowered or controlled by others. And, second, it is a way of reassuring oneself that one can have a subtle impact on—and control over—others by frustrating them.

Although Gerald was unusually perceptive about his pattern of demand-resistance, he didn't come to me seeking help with it. No obsessive ever has. Because they are unconscious behaviors, demand-sensitivity and demand-resistance almost always surface as patients and I address some more blatant and obvious problem, like depression or anxiety, work blocks, or commitment problems.

A small percentage of people, like Gerald, consciously recognize that they feel resentful, not only when someone tells them what to do, but when they feel even a subtle expectation or pressure. Some may have a reputation for being stubborn or oppositional. But it's far more common for demand-resistance to be nearly undetectable. *Inwardly,* the obsessive may sense some hesitancy when confronted by certain demands. "I get a tightness inside, a tightness in my gut," is how one patient described it. "I feel a suppressed anger." But often there are no external signs of this private turmoil. In other cases there are outward signs—procrastination or inability to stay with a task, for example—but the foot-dragger himself is bewildered and often dismayed by his inability to do what he consciously thinks he wants to do.

Demands and Work Blocks

I saw this in Jane, a fifty-one-year-old grant writer who came to me when she began to have trouble making progress on an assignment. Jane had a very productive work history, so this development surprised and upset her. She couldn't put her finger on any specific, conscious reason for her shutdown. As I questioned her, however, I learned that there *was* something different about the task on which Jane had gotten stuck.

Although she normally chose her own projects, this one had been assigned by her supervisor. At first Jane rejected the notion that this one factor could be the source of her trouble. She conceded that, by all standards, the assignment had been a reasonable one, and while she didn't find the project particularly exciting, neither could she truthfully say it was repugnant. And it clearly fell within her sphere of responsibility.

The more we talked, however, the more Jane began to express resentment toward her boss. "I don't really like him," she complained in one session. "He acts like a schoolteacher, and I react badly to that." Even after she finally forced herself to proceed with the project, she dreaded going to work every morning, and found herself silently curs-ing her boss after every interaction with him.

One day in my office, all these feelings came to a head. She shrugged and shook her head in confusion and frustration, her eyes filling with tears. Suddenly she thought of an argument with her husband earlier that day. When he had suggested she get rid of a broken dresser stored in their garage, she had angrily refused. "I think my resistance was really out of proportion," Jane told me. "It was an instinctual, almost visceral response. I was thinking, 'He's not going to take charge, not going to overpower me.' Some aspect of the domi-nance implied by his request reminded me of my mother. She used to overpower me. I was never able to do what *I* wanted. My way was never the right way. So I learned to just plant my feet, to refuse to budge."

Excited by this insight, Jane was now talking rapidly. She told me how she often had felt overwhelmed by her mother. "And I've felt the same way in therapy, that you're the adversary, making me do things I don't want to do. Like trying to get me to talk. And the only way to protect myself is to refuse. To clam up!" She soon was able to see how, with her boss and with me, her resentment and balking were not only unreasonable but self-damaging. That is, they were obstacles to what *she* wanted to do and were undermining her success (although she was totally unaware of their influence).

In this single session, Jane was suddenly able to see how the seeds of her demand-resistance probably were sown in her early relationship with her mother. She had learned to balk as a way of protecting herself from feeling steamrollered, first in that relationship and then else-where.

In view of Jane's story, you can see how demand-resistance has something in common with other obsessive traits such as thorough-ness, caution, and self-control. What begins as an effective means of self-protection becomes overdeveloped, indiscriminate, or automatic.

Ultimately this behavior becomes self-defeating, intruding on work, interpersonal relationships, and even leisure-time enjoyment.

THE RUINATION OF WORK

In the area of work, demand-resistance need not take the form of a full-blown block to be damaging. Work may simply weigh heavily on the obsessive, or she may have trouble concentrating. She may feel a festering resentment that saps her creativity and enthusiasm. Eventually she may have trouble motivating herself to do more than the minimum of what is expected of her. And her projects often wind up bearing the subtle mark of her resentment—coming in late, or with some small detail omitted, or in a form slightly different from what was requested.

You might be thinking that *every* employee sometimes resents being asked to do unpleasant tasks or having to carry out the wishes of superiors. That's true. The demand-resistant worker, however, is apt to sense demands that aren't even there, and to dread or drag his feet on tasks that aren't at all unpleasant. He's also likely to find himself feeling burdened by jobs he initially *wanted* to do. Even self-employed obsessives can experience inner demands as somehow coming from the outside. With no boss or supervisor to blame, they focus their resentment on the work itself, their clients, or their dependents (who are "making" them work).

When demand-resistance sabotages their on-the-job performance, many obsessives may start to feel demoralized because normally they take pride in their ability to work effectively. For many, the "solution" to this dismaying turn of events is to rationalize their resentment of, and alienation from, their work in ways that enhance rather than hurt their self-image. Since practically everyone regards conscientiousness as a virtue, that in itself often provides the perfect excuse. The obsessive tells himself he's a victim of exploited conscientiousness. "I bust my butt," he mutters inwardly. "I never miss a day, do a great job, sacrifice myself for the good of the company, and for what? No one appreciates my efforts and, worse, they're wasted, because the system is sloppy and inefficient." His feelings of victimization explain his negative attitude toward his work, and meanwhile the real culprit, his demand-resistance, goes undetected.

THE RUINATION OF LEISURE

Perhaps even sadder than its impact on his work is the damage demand-resistance can inflict on the obsessive's experience of his leisure-time activities. One painful consequence of the conversion of "wants" into "shoulds" is that at some point the obsessive comes to regard even potentially joyful activities as burdens. An obsessive may take up a project or hobby with a pleasant sense of anticipation. But somehow "I'd like to knit my husband a sweater" becomes "I really ought to work on that sweater"—something that *should* be done, exactly like an external demand. The person begins to slog through the project, rather than relaxing and enjoying the chance to be creative. Sometimes this unconscious resistance doesn't affect the actual performance of the task, but often it does. For instance, the person may begin procrastinating. In extreme cases it can lead to the abandonment of one hobby or personal goal after another.

Jan's behavior in this regard was classic. A single, forty-three-year-old traveling sales representative, she had been a successful child model—one saddled with an exploitative and manipulative mother. As an adult, Jan was deeply frustrated by her inability to carry out many personal projects. She was twenty to thirty pounds overweight and talked interminably about how much she wanted to slim down, but she couldn't make any progress toward this goal.

At one point, Jan seemed really excited about the prospect of getting involved with the Girl Scouts. Her prior involvement with such activities had always been fulfilling and exciting. Finally, after at least a year of anticipatory talk, she took the necessary steps and was accepted into the program, only to find herself overwhelmed by anxiety about the commitment she would be making and the demands her involvement with the program would place upon her time and freedom. "I don't understand why I'm fighting myself!" she told me tearfully. "I feel crazy sometimes, like I'm going in a circle and can't get out of it."

Even the simple task of writing down some of the things she wanted in life proved too difficult for Jan. When I suggested that she try this, she came back baffled by her inability to comply. "I get this idea that if I write something down that I *want,* I'll *have* to do what's on the list and I won't *want* to anymore. I get the feeling that as soon as I put a goal down on paper, it becomes an obligation!"

THE RUINATION OF RELATIONSHIPS

Besides work and spare-time activities, relationships also can suffer from the quirky pressures of demand-resistance. These pressures can interfere with everything from the start of a relationship to the maintenance of an ongoing one.

For instance, Judy happened to mention that she really liked another woman at the hospital where she worked. Yet she reported feeling "scared" by the woman's obvious friendliness. "I don't want to make a commitment of friendship to her right now. I don't want to set up expectations—I don't want her to come to expect my time or energy. I don't like to feel that people have claims on my time," Judy said. Even the thought of such demands made her feel panicky. "I just want out. I feel in danger of being smothered. To be around people, I have to do it on *my* terms instead of shared terms or their terms."

Obviously such feelings are likely to foil budding romantic relationships, too. Imagine the scenario that can develop when a demand-resistant bachelor finds himself at a small dinner party along with a few couples and an appealing, unattached young woman. At first he may well feel attracted to her. But as time passes he begins to sense some vague internal pressure to talk to her or even ask her out. He may sense that he's "supposed" to do something in a situation like this, or perhaps that the woman or his hosts expect him to act in a certain way.

The moment he feels this sense of expectation, he finds it difficult to act, regardless of how much he may consciously want to initiate conversation. He doesn't realize that the main obstacle is his automatic resistance, so he blames his hesitation on shyness, a fear of being shot down, or whatever other explanation is handy. You can see that at some point in this process he has lost sight of his own wishes. "I want" has gotten buried somewhere.

Despite these obstacles, he might be able to start dating the woman. But here again, problems may arise whenever he feels his date has expectations of him. For instance, he might sense a pressure to call at certain times, to spend certain days together, or to respond in kind to her expressions of affection. At these times he may balk, no matter how much he likes her or how badly he wishes he could show his positive feelings. She in turn is almost certain to mistake his apparent coolness for apathy or rejection.

Some of these behaviors may remind you of the commitment problems I discussed earlier. Problems with commitments and demand-resistance often coexist and sometimes they dovetail. They come from different underlying dynamics but can result in identical behavior, such as a reluctance to commit to marriage. This is a good example of two complementary motives being served by a single, final common behavioral pathway, or funnel, such as balking. Even more motives can be served by this same behavior. For example, many obsessives also have a fear of dependency, and of intimacy. It doesn't take much imagination to envision how these traits can also be served smoothly by a reluctance to become engaged. To me, this "funneling" is a remarkable illustration of how efficient a personality style can be.

Demand-resistance may plague even established relationships. It can sabotage isolated interpersonal exchanges, as it did for the patient who told me about a trip he had just taken with his wife. Even though he had liked their hotel, "When my wife raved about our room, I felt her statement as a demand that I agree with her. And I couldn't bring myself to say, 'Yes, I like it too.' "

Though this example seems fairly trivial, demand-resistance can easily inflict more serious damage on a well-established relationship. It can cause ongoing problems in a single area, as with Carla, the teacher who saw the slow deterioration of her sex life with her husband, or the damage may be more widespread. Sheila felt a lingering hurt and anger when she underwent major surgery and her husband, Gary, acted cool and distant. Why did he behave that way? Not because he didn't love her or was insensitive to her need for nurturance, but because he recoiled from the *expectation* that he give such nurturance.

Gary and Sheila found themselves squabbling chronically over Gary's uncommunicativeness. Gary described to me how tense and annoyed he felt every time his wife pressured him to talk to her more. "I agree to try, but I have this feeling that it's not by choice—that instead it's a marital obligation—and something about that just stops me cold. At one point I suggested that instead of saying, 'Let's talk,' she should just start talking, so that it wouldn't seem like such a demand."

Since his demand-resistance was unconscious, Gary blamed his lack of compliance with his wife on other factors. He told me that he didn't want to "set a precedent": "I feel if I *did* break the ice and open up a dialogue, it would be a constant expectation, that I'd have to sit and talk *every* night. I have this feeling that precedents are being set all the time, and they'll be thrown in my face in the future."

Although Gary expressed apparently sincere love and respect for his wife, he often felt irritated by her, a pattern I've seen repeatedly among resistive obsessives. Often they will harbor resentment toward the people, institutions, or rules they feel demand them to behave a certain way. Such people sometimes recognize this resentment, but just as often it is as unconscious as the whole process of perceiving demands and resisting them.

Are You Demand-Resistant?

Many people are consciously aware of and frustrated by the results of their demand-resistance—their chronic lateness, for example, or the trouble they have with expressing emotion. But I've found that such problems are harder to solve than other problems precisely because the underlying demand-resistance isn't as close to awareness as are some of the other obsessive traits—perfectionism, for instance. It takes more effort over a longer time to recognize one's demand-resistance and see clearly its effects. But progress is possible, and *becoming conscious of demand-resistance is the most crucial step.*

If you're obsessive, you are probably subject to many real demands. You have work to do, obligations to fulfill, rules and conventions to observe, standards you feel compelled to maintain. If you're as conscientious and hard-driving as most obsessives, you probably do what you have to do competently—even brilliantly.

You also doubtless approach some tasks with less than full enthusiasm. That doesn't mean you're demand-resistant. Virtually every one of us must do **some** things we don't want to do, and may seek to avoid them. If you really "have to" do something that's *objectively* onerous or distasteful, it's perfectly natural to drag your feet or to feel resentful as you complete the task. But that's not demand-resistance.

Demand-resistance is a chronic and automatic negative inner response to the perception of pressure, expectations, or demands (from within or without). It isn't easy to tell whether you are demand-resistant, and, if you are, whether this fact is causing you problems. But close self-observation will start you in the right direction.

In general, do you find yourself feeling reluctant or uneasy about complying when you feel that something—anything from returning a phone call to having sex—is expected of you? Do many of your activities feel like burdensome "shoulds" rather than things you actively want to do? Do friends or family members say you're contrary or oppositional?

Many obsessives can answer these questions with a simple *no.* While I've found that most obsessives are demand-*sensitive,* not as many seem to be demand-*resistant.* Some people seem to fulfill most of their perceived obligations happily and feel most comfortable when following the "rules," to which they are constantly alert.

If, on the other hand, you find you have to push yourself to do many of the things you "should" do, demand-resistance may well be undermining some aspects of your life. To become more certain, you need to recognize your inner rebellion each time you sense pressures, expectations, or demands. Once again, the key is sharpening your awareness of your own reactions. Observe your uneasy feeling when somebody asks you to have something ready by a given date. Notice your reluctance when it's time to begin the work. Watch yourself procrastinate. And ask yourself, What's making this so hard? Why am I hesitating?

Ask *why* you feel annoyed about having to carry out a legitimate request, why it's so difficult to do the things on your list, why going to Spanish class feels a little more burdensome each night. If you don't have a plausible answer to such questions, demand-resistance may be a problem for you. Even if you can come up with plausible reasons for balking, they don't necessarily rule out demand-resistance as the true culprit. Remember that this phenomenon often is deeply unconscious, and you might be rationalizing your behavior, so scrutinize your reasons carefully. I can't tell you how many times people have told me they avoid sex because they're just too tired in the evening, or they postpone projects because it isn't a good time to start them, or they are having trouble getting through tasks because the head of their department is obnoxious—only to discover later that even when the same conditions persist, they are able to change their attitudes and behavior.

Overcoming Demand-Resistance

The most important step in overcoming demand-resistance is *recognizing the demand-resistance consciously as it is happening.* Oddly, I find that many people are able to make changes as soon as they are able to recognize what's occurring. One patient, for example, told me, "It's just too much trouble, too overwhelming, to write the thank-you notes for my wedding gifts. It feels impossible!" But as soon as she said this, she laughed and said, "But it's *not* impossible! It's not all that terrible. It's crazy to tell myself that." She then went home and wrote the notes.

I wish it were always that easy to spot and discard a demand-resistant behavior. It isn't. (That particular patient just happened to be "ready.") But something else that should help you is to *start paying attention to the number of times you think, feel, or say "I should" or "I have to" rather than "I want."* If you are demand-resistant, this way of thinking is a self-protective habit that has grown out of proportion, causing you needless pain and undermining your sense of autonomy. You are *not* obligated to write any letter, complete your Spanish class, or have sex at any particular time, and thinking you are is preventing you from enjoying the positive aspects of these activities.

True, there are things you should—or even have to—do at work and in your personal life. But even these obligations are usually embedded in a context of something you wanted and freely chose and probably *still* want.

Let's say, for example, that you find yourself balking at writing a paper for a class you're taking, and if you don't write it, you won't be able to remain in the class. Ask yourself whether completing the class will move you closer to something you really want. If not, drop it and end the agony. But if it really *is* something you want, don't let that fact slip away. Think back to what motivated you to take the class originally. Remembering the bigger picture will help you. Writing the paper may indeed be a chore, but don't keep reminding yourself how awful it is. *You're making it much harder than it has to be.*

To change the pattern, you'll need to reconnect with the "I want" aspect of everything you do. Catch yourself thinking "I should" or "I have to," and challenge these thoughts. Stop telling yourself "I have to" unless you're certain that's the case. Don't let the ownership of your life slip away. Realize that even when you are pressured to do something, the decision to comply or not is *entirely yours.*

Kitty was able to come to this realization. The oldest of four children, she had been an extremely capable, responsible, and conscientious little girl. Her father, a university professor, was always exacting and critical, and her mother was overly protective and intrusive. She insisted that she and Kitty be confidantes, and hardly allowed for any distance between them. In their household it was expected that everyone's doors be left open; privacy was a rare commodity.

To protect her individual identity, Kitty became demand-resistant. When she first came to see me for depression, she was married to a man who had been the boy next door. Both families had taken the match for granted, and Kitty had never seriously considered other options. Although she was not profoundly dissatisfied with her marriage, her comments revealed her self-protective demand-resistance. In one session, for example, she told me "[My husband] and I had planned to go to a golf course driving range, and I decided against it at the last minute. That happens a lot! It makes him crazy. I don't know why I do it."

"Any ideas?" I asked.

"I think I've fallen into a pattern. When he suggests something, I automatically say no. Or if I do agree, I have a very negative attitude toward it. When he initiates something, I have to think about it. He will suggest we go sailing and I immediately say the bills have to be paid first. Even when they don't!"

"Sounds like you need to protect yourself, just like with your mother."

"I feel I might never really know my *self* unless I resist in this way."

Kitty and I worked on improving her ability to draw the line in her relationship with her parents, who were still actively involved in her life. She began to limit their contact with her; at first, for instance, she forced herself to be out of her house at the time when they typically called. Later on, although it terrified her to do so, she began to tell them things like "I'd rather not discuss that with you." We also focused on her automatic need to balk at perceived demands from her husband, and what this was costing her. Each time it came up, we discussed what the balking did for her versus how it harmed her, and we would scrutinize exactly how the process unfolded.

Although Kitty's marriage ultimately ended in divorce, her relationship with her parents has changed for the better. She has learned to tell her mother and father clearly what she wants from them (friendship and respect) and what she does *not* want (intrusions into her personal life, advice), and after a lot of upset, they have come to treat her more and more as an equal. It seems clear to me that as she has achieved successes with her parents, her sense of self has strengthened. As her sense of identity has solidified, her need to protect herself by balking has diminished. She's formed a new romantic relationship, and she reports to me that her resistance to her fiancé's legitimate expectations is very low. Yielding simply is not as "dangerous" as it once seemed to her. With her new sense of "Here's who I am and what I want and don't want," she doesn't feel as vulnerable to being overrun.

Little by little, an increased awareness of the "I want" part of the things you do—neglected for so long—will help you too to feel a more solid sense of who you are. Work won't feel as burdensome. You'll no longer feel like an unwilling victim. You'll bring more energy and creativity to your activities. Keep asking yourself, "What do I *want?*" about even the simplest things. I don't guarantee a clear answer every time, but it's amazing how often one will materialize if you practice.

SIX

Too Guarded

Of all forms of caution, caution in love is perhaps most fatal to true happiness.

—BERTRAND RUSSELL,
The Conquest of Happiness

It shouldn't be surprising that many obsessives tend to be too "guarded." If nothing else, *obsessives are alert to everything that might go wrong in life.* Unconsciously they yearn to protect themselves against all potential risk—an understandable desire. But, more than other people, obsessives often seem blind to the costs of too much "protection." And there are always costs.

Some degree of frugality is laudable, for example, but guarding your money also costs the time and energy wasted in comparison-shopping for even small items. It costs the pleasures forgone because they're "too frivolous," the generosity unexpressed because you "can't afford" to share.

Similarly, self-reliance is a good trait. But some obsessives are so uncomfortable with the idea of being dependent on anyone else that they guard their autonomy too fiercely. They may be unable to delegate work, for example, and must then spend the time and effort doing what someone else could do adequately.

Even more pernicious are the consequences of being overly guarded emotionally. This tendency can make it almost impossible to have mutually satisfying relationships. The need to hold yourself back from others can make you feel chronically constrained and tense; even worse, you may come to feel alone in the universe, unconnected, a stranger almost everywhere you go. The sense that no one truly knows you, or cares about you, is a sad and painful burden.

Guarded Against Intimacy

Let's first examine why anyone would shrink from achieving emotional closeness with others.

Humans generally are social creatures, valuing and seeking a sense of connection with others throughout their lives. Some therapists feel that this human striving for communion stems at least partly from a yearning to reestablish the infantile bond with the mother, who instantly "reads" and satisfies the infant's unspoken needs. Perhaps connecting with others is also a way to transcend our own mortality and finiteness. Without question, the experience of intimacy can open the way to feelings of unparalleled spiritual fulfillment. But intimacy has other consequences that many obsessives find frightening.

THE FEAR OF BEING FOUND OUT

For one thing, the closer you are to someone, the more likely he or she is to see all aspects of your personality—both the "good" traits and those you feel are unattractive or even shameful. Marvin, a successful banker, had little trouble meeting people and quickly winning their admiration. Yet he kept friends, acquaintances, and even lovers at a carefully controlled distance. "I'm afraid to let them really get to know me," he admitted in therapy one day. "I feel like a phony—that people will find out how inadequate I am underneath it all, and they'll be disgusted and reject me."

Marvin perceived a disparity between his public persona and his inner self, and it drove him to do things that ultimately caused him anguish. He yearned to feel closer to his girlfriend, but found himself setting up obstacles to intimacy. He often acted flippant with her, making ironic comments even during serious moments, and was careful not to let her see his feelings. "I must be afraid of something, because I keep holding her off," he confessed. "I'm afraid that once she sees beyond the image I'm projecting, she won't be as taken with me. I don't think she's aware of my negative qualities, like how insecure I really am." With her, as with other people, Marvin felt compelled to stay one step ahead of exposure. "I have to be the first one to jump, to leave, to push them away," he disclosed.

Many obsessives harbor such fears of being "found out." It's not that their virtuous public traits aren't "real." Most truly *are* honest, considerate, conscientious, committed to doing their very best. These admirable traits usually constitute a good part of their "real selves."

But early in childhood, many begin to perceive certain aspects of themselves in a less positive light. Often these are traits that family members either don't value or may actively disparage: aggressiveness, for instance, or sexiness. Gradually these traits are repressed or neglected in favor of other, more "acceptable" characteristics. Over time the obsessive comes to identify with and take pride in a set of traits very different from the repressed ones, and by adulthood he or she is likely to have become completely alienated from aims and impulses that clash with the approved behaviors. Obsessives are usually no longer conscious that some part of themselves yearns to be taken care of, for example, or occasionally feels hatred.

While they may not be conscious of precisely *what* they're hiding (from themselves and others), many obsessives sense that *something* terribly unacceptable lurks beneath the veneer, waiting to be "found out" by those who get close enough to see it. Some fear that the ill-defined "something" will be evidence that they are fundamentally "bad" or "evil." Others, like Marvin, may fear the discovery of specific foibles (such as insecurity) that contradict an image of perfection. Obsessives tell me, "I'm afraid that I'm *nothing* inside." Or boring. Or incompetent. Or uncreative. Even truly bright and accomplished people sometimes see themselves as impostors who have thus far managed to fool everyone but stand in constant danger of being exposed as unintelligent—a devastating possibility.

Invariably the disowned traits are *normal human qualities.* Yet invariably the person "feels" them—dimly, vaguely—to be something worse, something despicable. The very process of concealment somehow takes on a life of its own. Exposure itself comes to seem far more repugnant than whatever might be exposed.

FEAR OF TRUSTING

For many obsessives, another obstacle to intimacy is their difficulty with trusting. They fear that other people will let them down.

A patient named Elliot told me once that he couldn't think of anyone he trusted enough to talk to openly about his feelings.

"To some extent, I do talk to my family," he said. "But even with them, I'm reluctant to be too open. I worry that they'll use it against me later if I say anything really revealing."

"How would they use it against you?" I asked him.

"They could ridicule me. I tend to react strongly when I feel I'm being made fun of, which may make people even more likely to tease me."

Besides fearing that he might become the butt of jokes, Elliot also worried about being "manipulated," a concern that seemed to stem from his early childhood. "I always sensed hidden motivations in my parents. I felt they were trying to make me behave in a certain way or make certain choices, such as what I was going to be when I grew up. They wanted me to do what made *them* happy." These perceptions had damaged his ability to trust his parents and, by extension, others.

He had made one exception in the case of a professional mentor for whom he had worked for several years. When this man took away a major project and gave it to a new employee, Elliot felt devastated. "I worked harder for that guy than for anyone before or since," he disclosed, his face etched with lines of pain. "It was so unfair to give the work to this new person. I felt so angry and powerless and helpless to protect myself." His normal "protection" against hurt—cynicism and wariness—had failed him.

If there is a single unifying "theme" of obsessiveness, it is the desire to eliminate feelings of vulnerability and risk, and to gain instead a sense of safety and security. It stands to reason, then, that trust is one commodity in short supply among obsessives. Trust is a leap of faith that makes us vulnerable—to betrayal, exploitation, incompetence, chance, and the unexpected—a leap that flies in the face of guaranteed fail-safe passage.

To protect themselves against the vulnerability of trusting, obsessives tend to be wary. They doubt people's motives, honesty, and reliability. They doubt that others care for them as much as they say they do, and that these people will still care tomorrow. They doubt that their friends or colleagues will do what they say they will at the hour they say they'll do it.

They yearn to be able to put complete faith in their doctor, attorney, or stockbroker, but they wonder in spite of themselves about his or her competence, commitment to their case, and motives.

The anguish of being betrayed frightens some obsessives so much that they simply cannot allow themselves to be vulnerable to it. Sometimes this wariness persists after many years in a close relationship, such as marriage, even when the spouse has demonstrated trustworthiness. After twenty years of marriage, for example, Kyle and his wife were still arguing over his failure to express his love for her. "She's filled with twenty years of resentment and anger," he told me. "She says intimate communication with me is impossible, that I'm not willing to express my love or expose other feelings to her."

To me, Kyle acknowledged that he hadn't been a very trusting person, and his characteristic suspiciousness had intensified when he had been hurt several times after honestly disclosing his feelings. "People have betrayed me by repeating confidences; they've embarrassed me," he stated. But when I asked how often his wife in all their years together had betrayed his confidences, he confessed that he couldn't remember a single occasion. I asked if she'd ever done anything to make him seriously doubt her love, and he again had to admit the answer was no. Nonetheless, he still felt threatened by the idea of "opening up" to her.

FEAR OF DEPENDENCY

Besides the fear of exposure and the fear of trusting, intimacy poses another threat. The closer you get to someone, the more you come to need him or her. And this in itself unnerves many obsessives.

I often see this process unfold in therapy. Just when certain patients start to feel close to me, they may become critical of me or of the therapy. Sometimes they cancel appointments or even terminate our sessions altogether. Though many people don't recognize what underlies their behavior, some will admit, "I don't want to start to rely on you."

Part of their fear is that I may exploit or betray them. But there's another aspect to dependency that also bothers most obsessives. Dependency requires some sacrifice of autonomy, some loss of control over one's life. One patient put it this way: "When you depend on someone else, you lose your own strength. But you have to be your own strength—you have to control your own life—or you don't survive."

In other words, dependency, like trust, creates vulnerability. Moreover, the obsessive's all-or-nothing thinking magnifies the threat perceived in *any* amount of dependency: What if it were to lead to more and more dependency? Unconsciously the obsessive fears that he eventually will lose his very capacity to be self-sufficient. These people try to rely on others as little as possible.

Keeping a Distance

To protect themselves from the vulnerability of intimacy, many obsessives shy away from it in a variety of ways. For one thing, they typically tend to give other people as much physical space as possible. They rarely get too close when they're talking. Some shrink from too much direct eye contact—particularly when the conversation becomes personal.

A few have told me they feel trapped or smothered if their mates sleep too close to them. One patient said she wasn't totally comfortable when her husband hugged her. "I'm afraid that if he gets too close, he may be repulsed. Maybe I won't smell right or feel right. I won't measure up to what he expects." For some, the aversion to being touched is so strong it may cause them to shun physical therapists or doctors. Obviously, anxiety about physical closeness also can seriously impair one's fulfillment in sexual relationships.

Many obsessives do participate eagerly in the mechanics of sex, but avoid an emotional connection during physical intimacy. For instance, Kevin, a thirty-year-old librarian, complained that he and his wife didn't have sex often enough. Many factors contributed to this, but among them was a disparity in what each expected from intercourse. "What turns me on is a lustful, frenzied approach," Kevin said. "But what she finds erotic is a thoughtful, sentimental form of lovemaking. I don't want to do it her way." To show his love or affection for her during sex would have made him feel uncomfortably close to his wife.

THE MANY STYLES OF EMOTIONAL RESERVE

Mutually shared feelings bring people closer to each other. Conversely, guarding one's emotions is one of the best ways to keep one's distance, and obsessives hold themselves back emotionally in a variety of ways.

A certain stiff and formal quality distinguished Drake, a twenty-six-year-old engineer who was frustrated by his inability to sustain a romantic relationship. Drake conceded that his own insensitivity to signs of feminine interest had cost him a number of potential partners. "I miss out on cues. It's as if I walk around anesthetized. Sometimes, in fact, I'll pick up on the cues and act as if I didn't." Noticing flirtatious behavior and responding to it would expose him to the possibility of rejection. Furthermore, the thought of flirting back embarrassed him because such behavior clashed with the diffident posture Drake valued in himself. He came to see, however, that his obtuseness was costing him relationships.

Wanda, a nurse, presented herself in group therapy meetings as being very attuned to others, ever ready to help them. When others asked about *her* feelings, however, she invariably responded with generalities, or she would talk about former problems that she had resolved. One day two group members confronted her about this subtle form of guardedness. "You're vague," one person said. "You mirror what other people say, but you don't come out and express your own feelings." Another added that he felt he knew Wanda less than anyone else in the group. Finally Wanda acknowledged the truth of their accusations. "I'm afraid," she said, bursting into tears. "I'm afraid that if you get close, what's inside won't be good enough."

Some emotionally guarded obsessives seem arrogant or "stuck up," a façade they may only become aware of when people who get to know them reveal that this was their first impression. The obsessive is often very surprised to hear this; rather than being arrogant, he or she was feeling *anxious* in those initial encounters—afraid of being humiliated or rejected for some gaffe. But the aloof, cool stance was mistaken for conceit.

Other obsessives project charisma and warmth, but shut out even their close friends in certain fundamental ways. I think of Linda, the longtime chief assistant to a successful and charming television producer. Linda loved her job and was accustomed to putting in long hours with John; over the years they had shared both intense highs and bitter lows. They seemed to know each other's every little quirk. Yet, Linda confided to me, she didn't think of John as a friend. "I love many things about him and I know he cares about me," she said. "At work, we have an incredible rapport. But outside of the office, some part of him always seems to be slightly wary of me. After all these years, I feel as if I don't really know him."

Secretiveness

Sometimes efforts to maintain emotional distance can give one a secretive or cagy air. It can be quite obvious, as in the following exchange between a mother and her teenage son:

"How are you?"
"Okay."
"What's new?"
"Nothing."
"How's football?"
"Okay."

"Anything new with Joanne?"

"Mom!"

Obsessives can also be secretive about things other than their feelings. One patient told me that she was reluctant to have anyone come to her home; it was a part of her that she didn't want others to see. Other obsessives hide their opinions or conceal how much they earn or spend. Some patients say they hate the idea of neighbors observing their comings and goings, or that they would never want to be famous because of the inevitable loss of privacy.

Privacy generally is a highly prized commodity among obsessives. They're particularly apt to hide the fact they're in therapy. And even in the therapy relationship, many are very uncomfortable talking about things that are personal or "nobody's business."

THE NEED TO STAND ALONE

Earlier, I talked about how some obsessives fear being emotionally dependent on other people. As a "solution," they may try to become as self-reliant as possible, some even to the point of disavowing their emotional need for loved ones.

Margaret, for example, found herself unable to tell her husband, Jim, how much she missed him whenever he called home from business trips. When I asked what made it so difficult, she told me that she disliked feeling dependent on anyone. Pressed further, she admitted feeling afraid of being let down. As she struggled to explain this fear, an incident that occurred on her very first day of school flashed into her mind.

"Somebody took me to school but no one was there afterward to take me home. I remember walking outside and looking for my mom or somebody. But *nobody* was there! I ended up going to the home of one of my parents' friends, crying."

This wasn't the only time Margaret's parents failed her, and she eventually began to feel she couldn't count on them. Yet she yearned so deeply for their love that she repeatedly gave them chances to disprove her painful doubts. Each time she let herself trust them, they disappointed her bitterly. Later, her need to avoid a similar dependence upon and disappointment by others kept her at arm's length not only from Jim, but also from friends and colleagues. She felt painfully alone and craved intimacy, but could not risk it.

People who fear dependency often are extremely reluctant to ask their friends and loved ones for such things as time together, affection, sex, or emotional support. When I ask about this reluctance, at first patients will proudly cite their self-reliance. Eventually, additional explanations emerge.

For example, they feel that anyone who *really* cared about them would know what they need, and give it without being asked. Having to ask thus becomes evidence that they aren't truly loved. They also don't want to destroy the other person's opportunity to act spontaneously. "I'll never know if they would have offered it on their own," the obsessive thinks when a request is granted. "If I've had to ask, I can't tell if they're doing it because they care about me, or if they just feel obligated."

Asking poses other risks. The obsessive fears that the other party may secretly feel contemptuous of the "weakness" revealed by supplication. Worst of all, the request might be denied, a turn of events that would be devastating to the obsessive. First, it would confirm his doubts about the other person's concern for him. Second, it would expose with painful clarity the limits of the obsessive's control. Once again, the vulnerability is too great.

Several of these factors were operating in this extremely common situation recounted by Vivian. Though she had been involved with Ben for several years, she couldn't bring herself to initiate lovemaking. One day she mentioned that the two of them hadn't had sex in two weeks.

"We've both been exhausted. But somehow I also start thinking that it's a putdown. I guess I have this fantasy that a really sexually attractive person doesn't have to beg; that asking somehow confirms that I'm unattractive. There's also this feeling of yielding, giving in, subordinating myself, if I have to take the initiative. It's partly a problem with trust—that he might secretly be smirking over my caving in to him. And if he said no, I would feel crushed by the thought that he didn't find me attractive."

Some obsessives even avoid asking for much-needed assistance. They may, for instance, feel they have to be the one to fix anything needing repairs around the house. Or perhaps they insist on doing their own taxes, for fear that otherwise they'll forget how to do them, or they'll "lose track" of their financial affairs. Agnes was the thirty-five-year-old owner of a small business who couldn't bring herself to hire an office manager, even though she badly needed one and had to overwork terribly to handle all the tasks herself. "I'm afraid to give up the control," she said. "My basic instinct is not to depend on others." Further discussion revealed that this was a rationalization for Agnes's fear that the employee might become indispensable while Agnes would forget how to do the various tasks involved in running the office. If this were to happen, she'd be terribly vulnerable; a sudden departure by the secretary could mean disaster for her business.

Many obsessives hate to take medications. First they see the need for drugs as an acknowledgment that they already lack some degree of control. And, second, they fear they will become psychologically dependent on the drug and will have trouble giving it up.

In more extreme forms, a compulsive self-reliance can even make people uncomfortable about acquiring material possessions. Bennett, a twenty-five-year-old office manager, boasted that he owned so little he could pack up all his belongings and move in an hour. "I don't want to need anything or anyone."

Suspiciousness

In fact, Bennett wasn't alone. He lived with a girlfriend, but the ulterior motives he ascribed to her kept undermining his positive feelings for her. "I wonder if she isn't just trying to avoid being alone for the rest of her life," he said. "I also wonder if maybe she only *thinks* she loves me. Her self-esteem is pretty low, so how can she truly love somebody? I'm always in the detective mode, looking for the deeper meaning behind what she says."

Suspicions such as Bennett's are directly related to the fear of trusting. Obsessives often have trouble accepting that others simply like them, looking instead for what their partner is getting out of the relationship. Often they can't accept that someone who cares about them now will probably continue to care. They're cautious about what to reveal, for fear that the other person will hurt them with it later.

My obsessive patients doubt even *my* motives. When I'm exploring their thoughts and feelings, they feel I'm criticizing them, demonstrating my superiority, or exposing their deficiencies, and often they become quite defensive. Sometimes this is because their parents seemed critical or exploitative of them and they perceive me—through the warp of transference—in a similar role.

But obsessives also fear exploitation in more than just close relationships. I recently overheard a graphic example of this in a local photo shop, where a man was questioning the clerk about how his pictures would be processed. What if he didn't like the way they turned out? Did the business offer any sort of written guarantees? Who would be the judge of whether the pictures were of adequate quality and what would the criteria be, he demanded. He persisted, asking increasingly picayune questions, while his fear of "being taken" made him oblivious to the line of people rolling their eyes and expressing their exasperation behind him.

Guarded with Money

I find that many obsessives harbor a fear of being exploited financially—one component of an overall tendency to be guarded with money. Frugality may take many forms, including the following:

- A reluctance to spend money on anything but true necessities.
- The need to get the very best buy—regardless of how much time and effort are expended in shopping for it.
- A reluctance to disclose how much was spent for something—either because someone might judge that the buyer was "taken," or think he had a lot of money and an easy life, or that he had been unduly extravagant.
- A refusal to make personal loans—or, if a loan is made, the lender tracks it vigilantly—even if only in his own mind.
- Feelings of utter outrage if some product or service purchased turns out to be flawed.
- Pride in making one's possessions last a long time.

More than just the fear of being taken inspires the obsessive's tendency to be guarded with money. Many people learn early in childhood that saving is a virtue; they may come to associate it with other "good" characteristics such as self-denial and the postponement of pleasure for long-term rewards. A taboo against any frivolous expenditure is another possible factor, as is the perfectionistic fear of making a bad purchase. And obsessives, with their penchant for thinking far into the future, are all too aware that money spent now won't be available later (when they might need it more).

Guarded Against Spontaneity

Another form of interpersonal guardedness is the inability to act spontaneously. By definition, spontaneity means an absence of planning, anathema to most obsessives. "I'm not even sure *how* to take a risk," said fifty-year-old Jim. "Before I do anything, I think about it every which way. Before I buy something, I've gotten prices at five different places. I get things all figured out so I know which way to go, no matter what happens. I don't like to get anywhere close to situations where I don't have a lot of control; I can never just *be.*"

Most obsessives prefer to follow accepted social blueprints rather than risk the criticism, humiliation, or ridicule that might result from saying or doing the "wrong" thing. As children, they have a reputation for being more mature and serious than their peers. They rarely act silly.

When there aren't any guidelines, they feel uncomfortable. Many complain that they aren't good at small talk, and they may even avoid parties for that reason. Instead they choose their words slowly and carefully; even their casual conversations may seem scripted. One patient declared that unpremeditated talk scared her because of the possibility that "some kind of real feelings—weak feelings—may come out." She told me that she never talks candidly to her mother on the phone. She has to plan every word, in an often-futile attempt to block her mother's invariable criticism.

When the Guards Come Down

Though most obsessives have some trouble trusting, depending upon, and revealing themselves to other people, no one ever completely avoids any of those things. No matter how capable we are, modern life forces us to depend upon one another for such necessities as food, education, medical care, and much more. Some dependencies are so inescapable and routine (e.g., having to get water from the city supply or from bottled water vendors) that most people, obsessives included, don't think much about them. However, when circumstances arise that persuade one to acknowledge a dependency in a new area—to consult a doctor, for example, or seek help from an accountant—anxieties may arise. Discomfort also results when an area of guardedness breaks down inadvertently, as when some normally suppressed feeling, such as anger, suddenly surfaces.

If a guarded obsessive decides to place his trust in someone who betrays that trust, the betrayal can be devastating. It took Meredith a year to feel fully secure in her relationship and ready to make a real commitment to her boyfriend. But no sooner had she finally decided she could count on him than he dropped the bombshell that he was moving away to take another job. That night Meredith suffered a classic panic attack. "I woke up in terror. My heart was pounding; I couldn't get back to sleep. I felt chemically altered. It was so scary!" she told me. "I feel like a part of me has been destroyed. I try *so hard* to make sure that I won't be surprised, that I won't make a bad move. I didn't think he would betray me. But now I can't even trust him to care about me." Weeks passed before Meredith's anxiety subsided, and the relationship never recovered.

Guarded obsessives commonly view *any* betrayal of their trust as conclusive "proof" that their original guardedness was justified. "If I have a friend and he tells even a small white lie or is even slightly dishonest, I say 'Aha! He lied! That *proves* I can't trust him.' I subject him to unreasonable standards. He has to be one-hundred-percent trustworthy or I don't feel I can trust him at *all.*"

Becoming Less Guarded

Becoming less guarded is not something that can be "worked on" all alone, in the privacy of one's study. For all the pain that it can cause, a pattern of interpersonal guardedness is extremely difficult to change, and such change must take place within living, breathing relationships.

- Remind yourself that no one and nothing can be one-hundred-percent dependable. Other people—less obsessive people—understand this and still manage to trust and depend upon one another. Do you tell yourself that's because they just aren't as smart as you, that they simply don't see the risks or appreciate the dangers? Do you think they'll all be sorry someday? It's not that these people don't *see* the risks of opening themselves to others. Instead they know that many of the best things in life—such as a sense of connection and closeness with other people—are *worth* the risks.

- Don't be tripped up by your tendency to think in terms of extremes. No one is suggesting you should share intimate confidences with every stranger that you meet. A reasonable amount of discretion will provide you with *some* protection from hurt, rejection, and exploitation. But when it comes to guardedness, there is a middle ground, and people who find it are less lonely and isolated than those whose protective shells are too thick and hard.

- Try to be conscious of the fact that your guarded behavior is likely to *cause* the very rejection, isolation, and unloved feeling that you fear. Realize that other people are very apt to misinterpret your guardedness, taking it as a hurtful indication that something in *them* is causing you to hold yourself at a distance.

■ It takes determination and patience to become less guarded. Prepare yourself to see changes occur slowly. In individual and group therapy, guarded patients will sometimes begin this process unwittingly by revealing emotions in a "weak" moment. At such times they often feel humiliated and frightened. Sometimes they weep. But then they usually realize that nobody has rejected them. The world goes on. In fact, the others, sensing how difficult it is for them to open up, often respond with special empathy and warmth. Over time, the guarded person gradually is able to reveal more and more of the real self beneath the façade—the spontaneously experienced feelings and thoughts. And often, for the first time, he or she begins to experience what it's like to feel truly understood and still cared for—something that never before seemed possible.

Bert, for example, at first struck the other members of his therapy group as so cerebral and devoid of feelings that they were constantly irritated with him. To me, Bert had privately confided his need to be liked and accepted by the group, so he kept his competitiveness, anger, envy, and hostility tightly bottled.

Eventually he came to see how his guardedness, instead of protecting him, was repulsing the others and undermining his relationship with his girlfriend. He finally decided to try to let himself fully feel whatever was going on inside of him and then immediately to express it, even if those feelings scared or disgusted him or the group. At first, as he had predicted, a lot of anger and hostility emerged, and it sometimes stung the group members who happened to be on the receiving end. At times they were angry and hostile in response. But they continued to interact with Bert, in fact more than ever. They felt increasingly as if they were truly engaged in a relationship with him, and most members said it felt good. Bert, in turn, was astonished that no one rejected him.

As time passed, more of Bert's softer feelings began to emerge as well—affection and straightforward expressions of his fear and self-doubt. And Bert began to sense loving feelings, rather than animosity and estrangement, from the others. He eventually became a vital, committed member of the group, and he experienced similar changes outside of it. *He* became the one who would gently challenge other members who had trouble revealing themselves. He was the first to say he felt cheated by their avoidance of vulnerability. He was the one to express the desire for a closer relationship in the face of another's distance.

Bert also was able to transfer what he learned in the group to his other relationships; his girlfriend, in particular, was overwhelmed by the way their relationship blossomed as Bert was increasingly able to open up and share himself with her. He had been one of the most guarded patients I'd ever treated, but his ability to see what this was costing him, and his determination to have something more, enabled him to reshape his life.

SEVEN

The Thinkaholic: Worry, Rumination, and Doubt

I am plagued by doubts. What if everything is an illusion and nothing exists? In that case, I definitely overpaid for my carpets.
—WOODY ALLEN,
Without Feathers

Imagine yourself pedaling down a bike lane that runs beside a country highway. The morning sunlight warms the earth, and colorful flowers scent the air. But even in this rustic locale, traffic streams by. At times farm vehicles lumber beside you, filling your head with their noise. Faster-moving cars whiz by, and you can hear their whining engines far into the distance. Only for a few brief moments do you have the road to yourself, and only then can you savor the breeze, or hear the birds sing, or revel in the power of your hardworking muscles.

For many obsessives, life is a little like that journey down the country road. A steady stream of worries and painful thoughts distracts them from life's joys. In a sense, *they think too much:* it's nearly impossible for them to turn off the flow of concentrated observation, analysis, and reflection. "My mind is a regular worry machine," one woman said. "Sometimes I'll churn through every conceivable aspect of a problem, then I'll tell myself, 'That's enough,' and will try to shift to something more pleasant. A few minutes later my thoughts have crept right back to my worries. It's as if worrying is as automatic as breathing, something my mind keeps doing, no matter what."

Worry and rumination have few redeeming virtues. Once something bad has happened, ruminating over it only prolongs your pain. And worrying is at least as pernicious. If the object of your worry doesn't come to pass, you've suffered needlessly. And when misfortunes *do* occur, they will be just as irritating or devastating as they would have been even if you'd spent more time enjoying yourself and less time worrying. Worries trade chronic misery for the pallid hope of being a little less devastated.

The Obsessive Cognitive Style

Given these unhappy consequences, why do many obsessives devote so much time to worry and rumination? One element that predisposes them to this is their cognitive style.

Cognition is a general term that refers to our intellectual processes: paying attention, thinking, remembering, calculating, etc. *Cognitive styles* define the way we pay attention to things, the sorts of things that naturally draw our attention, and the way we "register" perceptions and thoughts.

The cognitive motto of obsessives might well be "Notice, Comprehend, Remember." They scan the world around them intently, directing their attention like a sharply focused searchlight. They typically read or observe things as if it were important to understand and remember the individual details rather than merely form an overall impression. They seem to listen more pointedly and concentrate more intensely than others do. It's as if the obsessive thinks he may *need* every scrap of information that comes his way.

Contrast that for a moment with a very different cognitive style, one that happens to be common to people with an urgent need to feel loved by or closely connected to others. Such people often take in the world in a more relaxed, passive, almost random way. They're much more attuned to the *emotions* generated by their experiences than to the *information* involved in them, and predictably, they tend to remember feelings very well, while having a poor memory for facts. Often this leads them or others to conclude, wrongly, that they're not particularly intelligent. Such people may also claim to have a poor sense of direction. But usually the true reason they have trouble finding their way back from a place is that they weren't thinking in the obsessive mode when they were on their way to their destination. Rather, they were *experiencing* the trip—the scenery, the conversation, the music on the radio. Most obsessives, on the other hand, are careful to make a mental map of where they're going—so they can be sure to find their way safely home.

Many obsessives are driven to acquire detailed information not just in areas impinging upon their immediate well-being but also about things that range well beyond their daily lives. This interest arises partly from a genuine pleasure in learning, partly from a desire to be viewed as a knowledgeable person, partly from the need to store data that might come in handy someday, and partly from the illusory sense of control that comes with knowledge of one's world.

Perhaps connected with this drive to know and remember everything is the obsessive's patented detail-mindedness. Many obsessives focus upon details at the expense of the "big picture," and have great difficulty prioritizing these perceptions. If given a Rorschach test, for example, they tend to discern lots of minutiae in the inkblots—small things that others generally overlook in favor of a more generalized impression. Obsessives often need to explain the significance of every aspect of the blot, just as they tend to feel compelled to make sense out of all they perceive and experience. Loose ends—disparate, jumbled fragments of information; unpredictable events; serendipity—

often are unsettling because they suggest chaos, the obsessive's nemesis. To feel in control, obsessives must somehow fit their perceptions and experiences into a comprehensible whole.

There is also another, simpler reason for this pursuit of comprehension. Obsessives generally strive to remember all the data they have acquired (and many in fact have an amazing memory for facts and trivia). Perceptions that have been sorted and organized into concepts are much easier to remember than are unrelated facts and data.

Consistent with all this, obsessives tend to be systematic thinkers, instantly and automatically sorting and analyzing the information they acquire so assiduously. As one patient put it, "Sure, I have feelings, but I'm mainly a 'head' person." Her chronic need to analyze whatever is happening to her, rather than just experiencing it, keeps her feelings safely in check.

UNDERLYING THE COGNITIVE STYLE

Several factors probably underlie the obsessive cognitive style. Constitutional differences—a matter of "wiring" or biochemistry—may predispose certain individuals to notice details, for instance, or to remember facts.

This style furthermore serves such central dynamics of the obsessive as vigilance, thoroughness, and perfectionism. If you have a chronic need to avoid risk or surprises, then an active, focused style of attention that enables you to remain watchful and alert will suit you best. Similarly, if your (unconscious) worldview is that your safety and control over life depend on your grasp of the universe, you will do your utmost to notice, comprehend, and remember as much as you can. You will be alert and observant, trying always to anticipate problems, and striving to remember names, dates, facts, and opinions.

Not only does an intellectual mastery over life create in the obsessive a sense of calm, but it has the very appealing side effect of bringing him the respect and admiration of those who find him so bright and competent. It also has practical value. The capacity for sharp, sustained concentration, for example, can significantly enhance your ability to master any number of skills, from playing the violin to programming computers. Detail-mindedness is an asset in everyone from police detectives to proofreaders, and a good memory for facts can serve you well in many contexts.

Unfortunately, some of these cognitive patterns may also create problems. When combined with rigidity, the penchant for "mental orderliness" can blind one to valuable new ideas. (We'll examine this problem more closely in the next chapter). Similarly, certain activities (such as nurturing children or listening to music) are at odds with too *much* detail-mindedness and objective analysis. Those traits may block your reception of intuitive insights or inhibit your ability to grasp the big picture.

I heard a vivid illustration of this from Charles, a physician patient of mine who had just undergone the oral board examination for certification in his specialty. One phase of the test required him to evaluate a man who had lost the ability to speak. Charles examined the patient and then presented his board examiners with observations that covered many details; he fielded even esoteric questions with ease. But throughout, he made no mention of the deep scar that disfigured the aphasic man's left temple (the result of a grave injury that almost certainly had *caused* the man's aphasia). The examiners finally asked about it. Charles *had,* of course, grasped the significance of the scar, but so eager was he to demonstrate his command of the fine neurological details of the case that he had failed to mention it.

The Wasteland of Worry

In the same way, mental tenacity may lead to pitfalls. If you generally find it hard to let go of ideas, you're almost certain to be troubled by worry, rumination, preoccupation, and/or doubt.

The wasteland wrought by worry is familiar territory to most obsessives. By worry, I mean thinking repetitively about a current or future problem *in a way that doesn't eventually lead to a solution.* Worry is unproductive by definition, and it seems to have a life of its own.

Almost everyone worries at least occasionally, and this is normal. When your child has pneumonia, for example, or when an international incident raises the specter of nuclear war, worrying is an appropriate response, even though you objectively understand that it will not affect the outcome.

But many obsessives worry *chronically.* At times, specific worries fill their consciousness; at other times, worry takes the form of a vague but foreboding presence that subtly drags the worrier down even as he or she goes about the various tasks of daily life. One patient put it this way: "It can be a beautiful day, but if I'm worrying, somehow everything seems shadowed. It's as if the worry blocks out the sun."

My patients seem to worry about almost everything, but among the concerns that preoccupy them most are the following:

- Day-to-day activities: "Will I be able to complete my project successfully? Will the restaurant forget my reservation? Will I have enough food for everyone who comes to the party?"

- Physical concerns: "Am I getting sick, losing my looks? Will I get in a car accident on the freeway?"

- Money: "How will I pay my bills? What about my future? What if the stock market crashes? Am I managing my money correctly?"

■ Loved ones: "Will my children be injured? Could my husband have a heart attack?"

Although those are some of the most common themes, worry-plagued individuals express an inexhaustible variety of concerns. One middle-aged businesswoman told me:

"I'm jealous of people who don't worry so much. I worry constantly. I have a pretty full life—enough to keep me worried about lots of things. I'm going to a book club tonight and I haven't finished the book and I'm worried that they'll think I'm not committed or just not intelligent. A friend is coming over to have a bite before we go, and I'm worried about the shape my house is in."

"How does it feel when you are worrying?"

"It feels awful!"

"So what makes you do it so much?"

"I think worrying about things at work probably makes me more effective."

"Really? Tell me about that."

"Well, maybe not the worrying, but being *conscious* does help me. But most of the time worrying is something I can't control. When I drive to an appointment, I'm worried I'll have an accident. I look at my watch every minute or so and worry that I won't be on time, or that I'll be too early. I worry that the person I'm meeting won't like me, or that I'll spill something, or that I'm not dressed appropriately. I worry that I'll run out of gas."

"Have you ever run out of gas?"

"Never," she replied, smiling ruefully.

As if worrying weren't painful enough, the tendency to think in all-or-nothing terms leads many obsessives to envision the very worst outcome possible for their concerns. Marcia, a twenty-nine-year-old music critic, described this very common experience:

"If I notice a strange blemish on my skin, I immediately think,

'What if it's cancer?' And I'm filled with all the dread and horror I would feel if I had already received the diagnosis, and part of my mind is racing ahead, wondering about cancer surgery, thinking about just how painful death from skin cancer is. Or when my husband is just a half hour late coming home from work, my mind invariably picks the very worst possibility to explain his delay. Like: what if he's been killed in a car crash?"

For most obsessives, the most awful things that have happened to them have occurred in their own minds.

Rumination: A Bitter Aftertaste

A slightly different—but equally painful—thought pattern is known as rumination: chronic or repetitive unproductive thinking about some *past* event or experience. You can ruminate about your own or someone else's errors or transgressions.

A recreation leader in her early thirties, Kristen felt devastated when a male co-worker failed to ask her out after having shown interest in her.

"My mind won't let go of it," she told me. "I just keep rehashing the interactions between us over and over again. I know I shouldn't feel rejected, and I'm embarrassed that I care so much about the whole episode, but at the same time, some part of me doesn't want to give it up. It's as if thinking about it might help me handle it better in the future."

Kenneth, a forty-year-old research physicist, became so upset about a used car he had uncharacteristically bought on impulse that he grew depressed, ultimately becoming convinced he would never sleep well as long as he owned it. Though it worked perfectly, Kenneth went over every inch of the car looking for flaws and worrying about what he would do if it malfunctioned. He suffered most, however, from his racking regret over having made the purchase at all. He always had sneered at buyers of used cars; whatever could have prompted him to buy one himself? Kenneth dwelt upon his "bad decision" so intensely that he felt exhausted and became unable to concentrate on his work.

Sometimes patients will ruminate over incidents that are insignificant to everyone but themselves. I could hear the pain in Matthew's voice, for example, when he told me how often he had chastised himself for failing to catch a fly ball at a company picnic held months earlier. Matthew had always prided himself on his athletic prowess, and at one time had even hoped to be a professional ballplayer. In the past, even when his sales had been lagging, his talented displays in the office baseball league had earned him admiration. Dropping the ball at the picnic made him feel—in that instant—that everyone suddenly saw him as just one of the crowd rather than as a star player, a fall from grace that burned in his memory, though in fact his colleagues hardly noticed it.

As with pathological worry, pathological rumination goes beyond the normal, expectable regrets or anger over unfortunate occurrences. And just as worry is a hypertrophy of some normal level of alertness and concern, rumination is a much-exaggerated variant of the healthy ability to remember damaging or unpleasant experiences well enough to avoid repeating them.

Preoccupation and Doubt

Two pitfalls related to worry and rumination also plague obsessives: the tendency to be preoccupied and the tendency to doubt.

Preoccupation simply means the inability to give one's full attention to the matter at hand, due to another matter being foremost in one's mind. Worry and rumination are forms of preoccupation, but they are not the only forms; the intruding thoughts need not be about a "problem," past or present. Consider, for example, the woman whose thoughts keep straying to her next day's schedule while she and her husband are making love. She may not be *worrying* about the upcoming events—merely thinking about them at an inappropriate time. But when those thoughts distract her, she obviously can't give her best to what she's doing, be that lovemaking, interacting with her professional colleagues, or reading to her child.

Doubting—not allowing yourself to feel certain about something—can darken your view of life. Many obsessives doubt their own judgment or performance, as well as the honesty, ability, or conscientiousness of others. Some are chronically pessimistic about nearly everything—they try to beware constantly of the possibility of failure or disappointment. As I've explained, this may also give them an illusion of control, since forecasting a negative outcome makes them feel they assessed the situation accurately.

Even when they're ahead by a lopsided margin, they refuse to let themselves become confident of victory. Contrast that with the non-obsessive person who, when almost sure of something, will usually feel and talk as if he were completely sure of it. The obsessive, on the other hand, will continue to experience and express doubt much longer—until the outcome is actually determined.

The Lure of Worry and Rumination

Powerful underlying forces make the obsessive cling to his painful thought patterns. For one thing, the tendency to worry is likely to be a central component of his self-image, and closely linked to other "good" qualities. Many obsessives associate worrying with being a serious, conscientious person, and on some level they view happy-go-lucky non-worriers as irresponsible.

Second, they probably feel that worry gives them some control over the object of their concern, somehow preparing them better for an upcoming event, for example. Maybe it will help them discover some protective action they can take (to prevent a party from being a failure, say, or to safeguard their family from violent crime). Worrying may be a form of "bracing oneself" to better withstand anything from romantic rejection to the Greenhouse Effect.

As well educated and intelligent as they often are, many obsessives also are superstitious about worry. If they worry about their spouse's plane crashing (so this twisted "reasoning" goes), maybe that will somehow keep it from happening. Worrying actively demonstrates their lack of presumptuousness; because they're not arrogantly assuming everything will go their way, the Cosmic Scorekeeper doesn't need to "teach them a lesson." Like all superstitions, this is an attempt to feel a sense of control over people and events that are essentially uncontrollable.

Similarly, most rumination carries with it a sense of retroactive control. By chastising themselves for some pitfall they should have foreseen (even if there's no way they really could have), they are denying the frightening reality that mistakes are inevitable.

Often, people who ruminate feel that if they dwell enough on their errors, or on bad things (done *by* them or *to* them)—if they can somehow sear these things into memory—then they can be *sure* not to let them happen again. A patient comes to mind who couldn't stop dwelling on his wife's infidelity, even years afterward. He tortured himself with painful fantasies of her sexual relationship with the other man, insisting that she tell him all the details, though this knowledge was almost unbearable to him. He remained in the marriage, but held fiercely to his anger for several essentially self-protective reasons. First, the angry feelings helped thwart any temptation to be close to his wife—and therefore vulnerable—again. Second, his clinging to the graphic mental pictures ensured that he wouldn't be as unprepared (and as devastated) if his wife ever betrayed him again. Finally, by refusing to put the past to rest, he kept his wife's infidelity fresh in *her* mind. He believed that her guilt feelings both punished her betrayal and made it more unlikely she would do it again.

The Costs of Worry and Rumination

Actually, this tactic often has the opposite effect. Failure to forgive and forget is much more apt to provoke resentment than it is to elicit a loving or nurturing response. And that's only one of the costs exacted by these destructive thought patterns.

Since both worry and rumination are unproductive by definition, they waste time and energy. All the time spent on either could be better used—either in some other activity or by concentrating more fully on the task at hand.

Worry and rumination also exact physical costs. They may deprive one of sleep, and some physicians believe that the feelings of tension and anxiety accompanying them can trigger (or worsen) other medical problems ranging from heart trouble to ulcers. They also tend to be mentally exhausting, not only draining one of intellectual energy but also robbing one of time that's much needed for creative rejuvenation. Although they're not physical acts, worry and rumination can be very strenuous.

Worst of all is the senseless emotional pain obsessives inflict on themselves with these thoughts. Chronic worriers or ruminators fail to enjoy many aspects of daily life because of this habit. They don't fully experience even pleasurable moments—time filled with family and friends, music, laughter—under the weight of their oppressive thoughts.

Abolishing Worry—A Practical Method

If you rationalize your worrying and ruminating by blaming them on external events—this or that professional problem, financial crisis, or potential social mishap—realize that *you're deluding yourself.* As soon as one problem is resolved or hurdle passed, you will find something new to worry or ruminate about. No matter how much money you earn, how good your health is, how satisfying your marriage is, or what other good fortune you enjoy, you'll always be unhappy. It is not external events that are causing your chronic unhappiness; *the problem is internal and self-created.* And this will never change unless you take active steps to change it.

If you're obsessive, you probably doubt you can change any of these "thinkaholic" patterns so ingrained in your personality. But this is one area in which I can offer direct, clear-cut advice that—followed conscientiously—is very likely to help.

It is a behavior therapy technique called *thought-stopping.* Before trying it, you must first be able to acknowledge that your worrying and ruminating are *voluntary actions.* External events don't "make" you worry; you've shaped yourself into a chronic worrier. Fortunately, with concerted attention and effort, you can moderate this destructive thought pattern.

The first step is to become more aware of your tendency to worry or ruminate each time it occurs. Negative thoughts at first may come so automatically that it will take you several minutes even to notice them. But with time you'll "catch" such thoughts closer and closer to their onset. The moment you do notice, say to yourself, "I'm doing it now. I'm worrying [or ruminating]." At the same time, try to examine how these thoughts make you feel—note your stomach tightening or your jaw beginning to tense up. Recognize that your emotional state is one of pain or discomfort, not relief or satisfaction. And notice how the worry or rumination is distracting you from more pleasant thoughts or something enjoyable in your immediate environment, or how it's sapping your attention and energy.

Once you can catch yourself worrying or ruminating, you're ready for the next step. Find a rubber band that fits comfortably around your wrist, and put it on. (For most people, newspaper rubber bands are ideal.) Wear it all day, every day.

Each time you find yourself worrying or ruminating, instead of paying attention to how painful it feels or what it's costing you, quickly pull the rubber band out an inch or two, let it snap back, and simultaneously say "Stop!" aloud. If you're afraid of being overheard, just say it to yourself, but give yourself a stern command. Inhale deeply, then relax and let the breath out slowly, telling yourself, "Worrying [or ruminating] won't help." Then refocus all your attention and energy onto whatever is at hand. Some people do their best worrying in the middle of the night, when there is no more pleasant or useful activity at hand. If this is the case, after you say, "Worrying won't help," focus all your attention on relaxing every muscle in your body, while imagining yourself in some peaceful, idyllic setting.

This entire thought-stopping process should take only about fifteen seconds. You may think it's too simple, too pat, or too superficial to have any effect on such a deeply ingrained behavior. It isn't. It has helped many people make significant changes.

Perhaps you are afraid that the rubber band will look silly or draw attention. Remember that the whole purpose of this exercise is to help you put things in perspective so that you can enjoy life more. Try to approach your self-consciousness, another self-defeating trait, in this same spirit.

Test the exercise for a month. You'll find that it won't jeopardize your job or ruin your relationships; it will improve them. Do this exercise as long as necessary for new habits to form. This usually takes months. However, several patients have told me that after the first month they rarely snap the rubber band anymore because just *looking* at it stops the worrying immediately.

Whether it takes several months or just one, you'll find the rewards well worth the effort. You'll be happier, more relaxed, and more able to enjoy the moment. You'll also find yourself relating better to others. If you're not mired in negative thoughts, you'll have more unfettered mental energy and attention available for family and friends, and they will notice and respond. They'll experience you as being more present and more connected with them. They will enjoy your company more, feel closer to you, and treat you accordingly.

EIGHT

Orderliness and Rigidity

To fall into a habit is to begin to cease to be.
—MIGUEL DE UNAMUNO,
Tragic Sense of Life

Remember Felix Unger of *The Odd Couple*? He was the archetypal obsessive—so perfectionistic that "I cooked myself out of a marriage," he complains in Neil Simon's stage play. "Nothing was ever right. . . . The minute she walked out of the kitchen I would recook everything." He was so tight-fisted with money that he literally made his wife keep track of every penny; so safety-conscious he wore a seatbelt at drive-in movies. But, more than anything else, Felix obviously—and comically—illustrated what it's like to be *too orderly*. His passion for cleanliness and organization drove his wife to seek divorce and his roommate to commit mayhem.

Felix's orderliness is an extreme example of a commendable trait found in many obsessives. Like Felix, some obsessives have a need for orderliness so great that it puts both them and others under undue stress. Furthermore, once they've established a certain order, whether in their surroundings, actions, or thoughts, they are loath to change it. They become rigid, and this rigidity can be very self-damaging.

Neat Freaks

I have a friend who fondly recalls a motto on a plaque that hung in her mother's home: "My House is Clean Enough to Be Healthy and Dirty Enough to be Happy." Its unspoken warning was that too much cleanliness leaves no room for enjoyment. The same goes for too much neatness. "I'm like a cat," one patient told me. "I spend most of my time on maintenance—grooming myself, keeping my things neat and clean and in good repair. There's not much time left over for *living.*"

That patient felt oppressed by the burden of maintaining an impeccable world. Others—the Felix Ungers of the world—may enjoy cleaning and straightening, but drive *others* to distraction with their insistence on orderliness. Such people can't resist tidying up while the party is still in progress, or chastising their children for the "mess" created by their play.

Felix-style "neat freaks" who can't tolerate *any* dust or disorder certainly exist, but it's far more common for obsessives' need for order to focus on certain areas. One patient, a retired military officer, volunteered at a library where he worked with materials relating to local history, his passion. He devoted hundreds of hours to cataloging and arranging the various books and papers, and he also happily spent a great deal of time cleaning and repairing items in the room where the collection was housed. Although this man didn't spend comparable time or energy cleaning and organizing anything in his own study at home, he was consumed by his volunteer work and felt upset when other people—such as library patrons!—disarranged things within his domain.

Rita also was not overly concerned about the neatness of her surroundings, but she was meticulous in the extreme about the organization of her computer files. When she began to write a book, she told herself that she needed to be able to find any given quote from among her voluminous material quickly, so she spent several months developing a complex system for cross-indexing all her interview notes. The result would have dazzled any data-processing specialist, but Rita later admitted that she rarely used the cross-indexing features, and that all the time spent developing the files contributed to her delivering the manuscript almost a year behind schedule.

Straightening, classifying, and otherwise organizing things are favorite activities for many obsessives. Such tasks clearly have intrinsic value; it's easier to find and use possessions or pieces of information if they're arranged in good order. But these activities also may impart a symbolic reassurance that one can order life in its greater aspects— that the unexpected catastrophe can be avoided.

Doing Everything "In Order"

Besides organizing their physical surroundings, obsessives also tend to be orderly about their *activities*—doing them in a methodical manner rather than haphazardly. A given person might have a precise pattern for doing housekeeping chores, or might always sit down with the newspaper at the same time every day, reading the various sections in a particular sequence. Another might have a well-fixed morning work routine—say, insisting on first returning all phone messages before doing anything else, rather than every day trying to decide anew what activity is most urgent.

Being organized usually enhances effectiveness, allowing one to use time more efficiently. And when procedures are codified, others are enabled to duplicate certain activities quickly and correctly. Finally, routines (in which the same sequence of events is automatically repeated) can free you from having to think about humdrum chores. When you brush your teeth in the same way every day, for instance, the act seems effortless.

But the obsessive's orderliness stems partly from his need for perfection, thoroughness, and control. When this is the case, one's need for order will go beyond its adaptive value to reach self-defeating proportions.

There's a scene in Anne Tyler's novel *The Accidental Tourist* that nicely illustrates this. The protagonist, Macon Leary, who "above all else . . . was an orderly man," recalls taking his young son, Ethan, to the movies.

"I got the tickets," he heard Ethan say. "And they're opening the doors in five minutes."

"All right," Macon told him, "let's plan our strategy."

"Strategy?"

"Where we're going to sit."

"Why would we need strategy for that?"

"It's you who asked me to see this movie, Ethan. I would think you'd take an interest in where you're sitting. Now, here's my plan. You go around to that line on the left. Count the little kids. I'll count the line on the right."

"Aw, Dad—"

"Do you want to sit next to some noisy little kid?"

"Well, no."

"And which do you prefer: an aisle seat?"

"I don't care."

"Aisle, Ethan? Or middle of the row? You must have some opinion."

"Not really."

"Middle of the row?"

"It doesn't make any difference."

"Ethan. It makes a great deal of difference. Aisle, you can get out quicker. So if you plan to buy a snack or go to the restroom, you'll want to sit on the aisle. On the other hand, everyone'll be squeezing past you there. So if you don't think you'll be leaving your seat, then I suggest—"

"Aw, Dad, for Christ's sake!" Ethan said.

145

Macon's urge to "organize" his moviegoing experience, his imperative to plan every facet, transforms it into something serious—something very like work.

The teacher or writer who feels compelled to present material in neat, perfectly logical fashion may do so at the cost of boring his or her audience; the excessive orderliness is apt to exclude any humor, spontaneity, or creativity. Yet another drawback of excessive orderliness is that it sometimes takes more time and effort than the task deserves.

Too Rigid

The greatest danger of the obsessive's passion for order, however, results when it combines with another typical trait: the tendency to resist change, to be rigid. This marriage of orderliness with rigidity was illustrated by a patient of mine named Tim. An enthusiastic jogger who ran at least four times a week, Tim always ran for the same length of time along the exact same route. At one point he told me how bored he was by this unvarying routine, but because he was comfortable with it, he really didn't consider an alternate route. "I know exactly where I'm going. And it fits the time allotment exactly," he said.

Tim offered other rationalizations, but when I suggested good solutions to each of these problems, it became clear that maintaining the order itself had become some sort of imperative. Something about his running routine had taken on a life of its own. Somehow it had come to be the "right" way, and any deviation simply felt uncomfortable, as if he were breaking some rule.

CAUGHT IN A RUT

Tim had fallen into a rut: a routine so strong that he resisted deviating from it even when he knew that it would serve him well to do so—even when he *planned* to do so. Obsessives are unusually prone to ruts. Their slip into some inflexible behavioral pattern may occur gradually, but it can also occur with astonishing speed. One patient confessed that he went to the same barber he had chanced upon when he first arrived in town, even though he had since learned of others who were better, cheaper, and more convenient. A dental student named Norma found that if she studied for a certain amount of time for one class, she felt she had to do the same amount for the next class, even if it wasn't really necessary. When such rigidity combined with all-or-nothing thinking, it made things even worse. "Whenever I fall off my routine, I feel terrible, like I've messed up so badly that it's not worth studying at all," she said. "And it's likely to take me a while to get going again."

Ruts have many other drawbacks. For one thing, they can cause you to miss out on valuable opportunities. I think of the great pianist Vladimir Horowitz, who reportedly loved great restaurants but, no matter where he was, ordered the same dinner: soup, sole, boiled potato, asparagus vinaigrette, and creme caramel. Think of all the great veal dishes that he missed out on, the Chinese food!

Adhering too inflexibly to your routine can subject both you and the people around you to unnecessary pressure. I saw this in Eleanor, a housewife who was driven to keep her house in impeccable order, hewing to a fixed schedule of chores throughout the day. For instance, she liked to get all the laundry done by eleven each morning. She had to serve her home-cooked meals precisely on time, and if the family sat down to eat even a few minutes late, she felt vexed—even if the delay caused no particular problems. Always in a hurry, Eleanor usually wore a serious expression on her face. She resented any interruption—a call from a relative, a request from one of her children for a ride to the park—as an intrusion that could throw her whole schedule into disarray.

Above all, ruts are boring. Day after day to buy the same kind of sandwich from the same deli; to go to the movies every Saturday night; to make love always in the same position—such routines may relieve you of some amount of risk and effort, but they also drain life of its color and spontaneity.

When circumstances or other people *force* the habit-bound obsessive to change his pattern, he often will feel annoyed or anxious. When I moved to a new office, a patient named Muriel made several disparaging comments about it, even though the new location was actually more convenient for her. When I questioned her, she admitted that the move had bothered her.

"Any idea why?"

"I was used to the other place. I felt comfortable going there. Changing it feels like we're rocking the boat, and my natural inclination is to resist doing that."

Another patient, an eminent attorney, was in the habit of opening his mail as soon as he got home, and paying any bills on the spot. He explained that he had learned through hard experience that if he didn't do this as soon as he walked in the door, he was apt to misplace the bills and overlook paying them. So he doggedly wanted to stick to his routine one afternoon when he and his wife returned home—even though they had a group of friends in tow. "Martha insisted that I ignore the mail and get everyone a drink, and we almost wound up fighting about it. I finally humored her, but I felt extremely irritated."

A SLAVE TO "THE RULES"

A second important way in which obsessives can become too rigid about their orderliness is by deferring excessively to outside authorities or strictures. Rules and regulations, ethical codes, written procedures, all help to organize and smooth out complex human interactions. But when such guidelines take on a life of their own and become more important than the reasons for instituting them, they can be more destructive than helpful.

Some obsessives feel compelled to follow recipes to the letter, for example, even when a substitute for a hard-to-find ingredient would work out fine. And if these people are forced to deviate from the recipe, they often are unhappy with the resulting dish, no matter how delicious. Other people may fail to question "expert" advice even when there's clearly reason to do so. One woman, for example, continued taking a new medication throughout the weekend, even though it was obviously causing her unpleasant and unexpected side effects. She later told me that she didn't want to "bother" me with a question about the drug, though I had urged her to call at any time.

Seven-year-old Adam's underlying respect for most rules is so intense that his parents often have to urge him not to dwell upon them so singlemindedly. They recently gave me this account of a Sunday afternoon outing with him.

"First he insisted that we leave really early so that we wouldn't be late for the play we were going to see. While waiting for it to start, we spotted some friends, and they moved up to empty seats behind us in order to chat. In fact, they stayed there when the show started, and Adam was so *worried* that the assigned seatholders would arrive and 'catch' our friends where they weren't supposed to be. We had to keep reassuring him that nothing catastrophic would happen.

"After the show, we all strolled to the merry-go-round, and the moment he was on a horse, Adam began scanning for the ticket-taker. He was visibly tense when the ride started and he hadn't yet handed over his ticket. Again, we had to tell him to relax—that even if the man somehow overlooked the ticket, the world wouldn't end."

Adam may someday have to fight the urge to join the ranks of the overzealous rule-enforcers. We've all encountered such people: the bureaucrat who insists that "procedures" be followed even when they're clearly ludicrous, or the hospital admissions clerk who demands answers to dozens of trivial questions before allowing the suffering patient access to medical aid. A patient named Karen complained that her father had shared this mentality. "When I was seven years old, the rule was that I had to be in bed by 8:30 P.M., and he was just a bear about enforcing it! I even remember him making me go to bed when we had company over, with kids my age. He said I needed my sleep; that I would be cranky the next day if I stayed up late. As it turned out, I just lay there awake for hours, hating him."

Mental Orderliness and Rigidity

Another kind of orderliness that applies to the obsessive person is a sort of *mental* neatness. Despite their boundless capacity for doubt, most obsessives crave an unambiguous "ordering" of their various experiences. They yearn for a clear comprehension of things; life's ambiguities make them uncomfortable and impatient. Some feel unsettled or even annoyed if they don't completely understand every detail of a movie or lecture, focusing on that to the exclusion of the other, more enjoyable aspects. Many are more at ease reading a biography or a technical book than something more abstract, like poetry. Obsessives' friends and spouses often refer to them as "analytical."

As with other aspects of orderliness, the capacity for mental organization—sorting packages of data into the categories where they "belong"—has obvious survival value. But equally essential to navigating effectively through life is the ability to change one's ideas and opinions when conditions change or new information becomes available. And this is where many obsessives have difficulty. They are hobbled by a mental rigidity that makes it hard for them to revise their thoughts and opinions even when it would serve them better to do so.

A commonplace example of the impact of mental rigidity can be seen in the person who misplaces a shopping list and then spends more time looking for it than it would take simply to start afresh and reformulate a new list.

In its most virulent form, rigid thinking can show up as stubbornness, narrow-mindedness, resistance to progress and growth. I had this conversation with Harold, a forty-seven-year-old postal inspector, who one day declared, "I avoid New Yorkers. I can't stand them."

"What is it that you don't like?" I asked.

"They're arrogant, pushy, insensitive. My cousin Jim is a good example."

"But didn't you tell me that your friend Fred is also from New York?"

"Yes. So?"

"You said you liked him very much, that he's kind and sensitive."

"He is!"

"So some New Yorkers aren't so bad?"

"But they're so damned arrogant and aggressive."

Conversation with such a person can be frustrating. When I talk to Harold, I often have the sense that he's simply not listening to me. And in a sense he's not, because to truly hear my point of view would threaten him. Even when he has a hunch that his understanding of a given topic may be inaccurate, he resists considering any other viewpoint. First, acknowledging the merits of the other viewpoint might look too much like an admission of error, and would give others the idea that he was unsure of himself. Or what if he wasn't capable of understanding the newer viewpoint? And even if he did understand it and agree with it, he might be unable to integrate it without having to change his whole belief system—a system that he depends on for a sense of calm and control.

Even when the subject in question isn't very significant (e.g., his feelings about New Yorkers), it's symbolically important. Having a solid understanding of things buttresses his illusion of control. In a way, to comprehend life is to be in control of it. If, on the other hand, his ideas in some small matter need revision, where will it end? Which other pat ideas are flawed? Are there *any* that aren't? Mentally rigid obsessives have an underlying fear that they're on the verge of spinning out of control, with nothing to hold on to.

Even when it doesn't take as extreme a form as it did with Harold, mental rigidity is usually a liability. It tends to choke off creativity, as was the case for Lena, a thirty-five-year-old architect. "When I first started working on design projects in school, I found that once I had come up with an approach, I would be really resistant to considering any other solutions. I'd get very defensive about my first idea. It took me a long time to realize that I could generate *several* good ideas. With some difficulty, I've learned to prevent myself from becoming too attached to any of them, at least initially. I've discovered that if I become emotionally attached to one idea, I'll close off my mind to other possibilities, even when I'm confronted with the fact that my first idea is flawed."

Finally, rigid thinking may also take the form of rigid expectations. When things don't go exactly as the obsessive expected them to go, she tends to react with inordinate disappointment or even rage. Jill, a twenty-six-year-old travel agent, provided this example about her husband:

"If Bill says he's going to roast a chicken for dinner, and then he instead surprises me with lasagna, it's likely to drive me up a wall. It's not that I don't like lasagna. I do. But I was *counting* on having the chicken. I feel so disappointed, and even *angry* that I won't get what I was expecting."

Carrying through with what one had anticipated becomes a strong motivator, even when the situation warrants changing one's plans. Jill said, "If I decide to spend a Sunday afternoon working on minor chores, and on Sunday morning I get a call from friends, inviting me out, more often than not my immediate reaction is to say I'm already busy and beg off. I may feel sad that I'm missing out on the fun, but once I've set my course, it's very hard to change it."

Toward a More Flexible Orderliness

Chances are you don't think of yourself as an excessively orderly or rigid person. Almost no one does. But consider carefully the following questions:

- Do your demands for neatness make family members tense or inhibited around you?
- Do your children ever feel pressured (by you) to do everything just so?
- At work, has your resistance to new ideas or methods ever stifled your growth or inhibited development of your product or service?
- Is it hard for you to enjoy an unexpected visit or call from a friend or family members because you had anticipated doing something else in that time?
- Do you wish you could be more spontaneous?
- Is it hard for you to start work or fall asleep until your surroundings are arranged meticulously?
- Do you get upset when unforeseen contingencies disrupt your routine?
- Keeping things extremely organized takes a lot of time. Is your need for neatness and order contributing to your feeling chronically overburdened?
- Does your tendency to get into routines make aspects of your life such as lovemaking, meals, or weekends boring and predictable?

- Do you wish you could be more creative?
- Do you find yourself increasingly alienated from current social and political ideas, music, or clothing styles because they conflict with how things used to be?

Excessive orderliness or rigidity can manifest itself in a variety of ways. If you can pinpoint difficulties these traits are causing you, you will be well on the way to making some improvements.

Catch yourself straightening, organizing, cleaning, or filing far beyond what's necessary or functional. Think of a clock ticking away the precious seconds of your life. Add up all those wasted moments— the weeks, months, or even years—time that you might have spent creatively, productively, or just plain having fun.

Notice yourself rejecting spontaneous ideas, suggestions, or activities simply because they break your stride. You have paid dearly for this automatic veto.

Mark well how a vacation or an evening out can be ruined simply because things don't go as planned. Observe yourself doing the same things in the same old way time after time, while at the same time yearning for freshness, excitement, creativity, and nuance in your life.

Take note each time you insist that a family member or employee do things exactly in the fashion *you* prefer, rather than in his or her own style or order. And ask yourself if having it done your way is worth the damage to the relationship.

Don't stop there. In each case, ask yourself what would be so terrible about making a small change. If modifying your demands slightly won't have dangerous repercussions, try doing so. I seriously doubt you will become completely disorganized or unable to function effectively as a result of becoming a bit less orderly or rigid. It's far more likely you'll become *more* productive as well as more creative, easier to get along with, more relaxed, and generally happier.

NINE

Too Driven

A man who loves life intensely must be always jealous of the few exquisite moments of leisure that he has. . . . His hours of fishing must be as sacred as his hours of business.

—LIN YUTANG,
The Importance of Living

Work permeates every moment of Natalie's carefully planned schedule. An ambitious public prosecutor, she rises before dawn so she can arrive at her office by seven-thirty and take advantage of the hour of calm before the day-long flood of calls and meetings begins. Because she has a seven-year-old child, she disciplines herself to be home no later than six, but she often finds it hard to shift her attention from the day's professional concerns. She confesses, "All too often, I feel distracted, or irritable over work I've left undone." After dinner with her family, she invariably works for a few more hours. "During trials it really gets crazy. I become so wrapped up in the important cases that I don't get much sleep, and of course everything else in my life suffers. Thank God, those periods only last for so long." Even when she's not trying a case, however, "I'm stretched awfully thin," she admits. "My family would like to see more of me, but I always have lists upon lists of things that have to be done. I get three weeks' vacation every year, but somehow I never seem to be able to get away for more than a few days!" Even though her supervisor has urged her to drive herself less furiously, Natalie can't really imagine cutting back her work hours. "My job is like a vortex," she says flatly. "It draws me in."

The Obsessive Workaholic

Most people would call Natalie a "workaholic." Although this is not a psychiatric term, the recently minted word aptly describes a person having a compulsive need to work. It applies to many obsessives. For them, work represents much more than just a way to earn a living; it's the central axis around which everything else revolves.

Workaholism is more than just a matter of long hours. No one, for example, would label as a workaholic the impoverished immigrant who sews for eighteen hours a day. She probably has no psychological *need* to work so hard, and one assumes that were she to win the lottery, she would work less. When most people call someone a workaholic, they are implying that the person works significantly more than he or she has to or is even expected to.

My own definition is that *a workaholic is someone who voluntarily devotes practically every waking hour to either doing or thinking about some form of work* (though he may not realize his actions are voluntary). This incorporates a very broad range of overly driven behavior. Let's look at some of the varieties of workaholism.

The Classic Workaholic

Workaholics like Natalie are notable for the sheer number of hours they devote to their careers. Sometimes they'll describe themselves as workaholics, though even the most work-addicted individuals often reject that term because of its negative connotations. "I'm just a very hard worker," they'll say, adding—sometimes—that their work happens to be the most important thing in their lives.

While some work as many as sixty, seventy, or even eighty hours a week, they don't necessarily spend all that time physically on the job. With the advent of such tools as personal computers, car phones, and home fax machines, work has increasingly invaded the traditional bastions of leisure. And many types of work can be done at home without any high-tech gear. Kathleen, a successful literary agent, commonly leaves her office by 6:00 P.M., but devotes hours every night and most weekends to her daunting reading load: four newspapers a day, hundreds of monthly magazines, and an unending pile of manuscripts. "I find a lot of good book ideas in all that reading, but it's really a chore. I virtually never have a chance to read for pleasure anymore. I used to *love* reading," she says sadly. "But now it's a grind."

Even when the workaholic is not actively engaged in job-related tasks, it's common for this sort of person to be dogged by thoughts and worries about his professional responsibilities. "I never feel free," declared Nora, a beleaguered hospital pathology lab director. "I'll wake up at night and lie there fretting about the project I'm coordinating. I hate doing it because I know I'll be less sharp than I should be the next day, but I can't help it."

"You get sort of revved up and wired, and it's very hard to turn it off," stated one workaholic stock analyst. "I've learned to be careful not to work very late—say past ten. Because if I do, I can't get to sleep. And then I'm exhausted and irritable the next day."

157

Some work addicts consciously yearn for time off or complain about being overworked, but find themselves resisting opportunities to take vacations or other time away from work. They may even announce plans to do so, and then find themselves slipping right back into their overloaded schedules. Georgia, a management consultant, looked forward eagerly to a three-month maternity leave when she became pregnant with her first child. But just three weeks after the birth of her daughter, she felt the onset of cabin fever. "I've always had the kind of job where I was surrounded by people who need me, and I really missed that. I felt lonely." She began accepting calls from her office, and within a few weeks she was working every day, holding meetings in her apartment, with her infant sleeping close by.

In his book *Work Addiction,* Bryan E. Robinson confides that he contemptuously thought his colleagues were lazy when they looked forward to Thanksgiving and Christmas holidays. Such feelings of superiority, while sometimes hidden, are common among workaholics. Or, like the fabled hardworking ants, the work addict also may see the easygoing grasshoppers around him as setting themselves up for some inevitable disaster.

However, don't get the idea that if someone does enjoy his or her vacations, it's proof that he or she is not a workaholic. I find that many workaholics are able to take pleasure in their vacations *once they can get away.* Getting away is the hard part. Workaholics tend to postpone taking time off "until next year," or "until we get over this rough spell." They're great rationalizers, telling themselves such things as, "I'll have more money next year," or "I didn't expect this upturn [or downturn] in business," or "I'll be less pressured and will enjoy myself more if I wait a bit." They genuinely don't see that they could take the time off, if only they would consider the idea in good faith.

WHEN THE WORKAHOLIC CAN'T WORK

When outside forces threaten to prevent them from working, some workaholics go to ludicrous lengths to overcome the impediment. During the 1977 New York blackout, for instance, hundreds of people flocked to their job sites in defiance of pleas from city officials that they stay home. "I found them pacing impatiently outside their offices, demanding to be allowed to enter, even if reaching their desks would require climbing thirty flights of stairs," wrote psychologist Marilyn Machlowitz in her 1980 study, *Workaholics.*

If he is actually prevented from working—by illness or a job loss, or by a work block such as those we discussed earlier—then the obsessive's level of anxiety is almost certain to increase and his self-image to suffer. For many obsessive workaholics, their sense of identity depends far too much on their professional role, and if they're seen as anything less than outstanding in their chosen field, they may feel as if they're *nothing*. A serious depression may ensue.

WORKAHOLICS AND DENIAL

Some of my workaholic patients acknowledge that they set their own frenetic pace. But I more commonly hear a different refrain: "I'm not a workaholic! I wish I had more free time, but I feel overwhelmed by all that I have to do." Like the immigrant seamstress, these people claim that they "have to" work as much as they do because they'll lose their jobs if they don't. Or their clients need them. Or they've got to take advantage of a particular economic or professional opportunity. Is this sort of person a workaholic?

That isn't always immediately apparent. By my definition, the key is the extent to which the person is in fact *choosing* to overwork, despite his protestations. And the amount of time any person devotes to work versus leisure depends on a complex mix of variables.

For example, there's evidence that *most* Americans today work longer hours than they did fifteen years ago. One 1989 survey by pollster Louis Harris, for instance, indicated that the amount of leisure time enjoyed by the average American has shrunk 37 percent since 1973, with the average work week (including commute time) going from forty-one to forty-seven hours. Studies invariably show that people in management or entrepreneurial roles work even longer, and at some companies, chronic long hours are a prerequisite for getting ahead.

Sometimes people have virtually no choice but to yield to unusual work pressures for a limited time period. I think of the software engineer who must put in eighty hours a week during the final stage of debugging a major project, or the magazine editor who works twenty hours a day when the monthly deadline draws close.

Clearly, strong external forces can drive one to overwork. But for other individuals, the forces impelling them comes from within.

Jeffrey, for instance, grumbled constantly about all he had to do as editor of a weekly newspaper. Weekdays found him toiling ten to twelve hours at his office, and he also devoted either Saturday or Sunday to professional matters. Several times a week he scheduled business dinners, and he invariably ate lunch at his desk. Even in his off hours, his mind rarely strayed from some aspect of his job. Jeffrey complained to friends about the impact of all this work on his social life, and he occasionally seemed to resent the extent to which his job dominated his life.

In fact his boss eventually became so concerned about the possibility of his star employee's burning out that he worked out a plan under which Jeffrey didn't have to come into the office on Tuesdays, the slowest day of the week. The boss further insisted that he wasn't to work at home on those days, but was to read, relax, and recuperate. Instead of leaping at this offer, however, Jeffrey pointed out all the things that wouldn't get done, or wouldn't be done well enough, if he took this day off. Eventually he did yield, but within a few months he had reverted to scheduling at least a few hours of work on his mandatory "free day." Contrary to his words, Jeffrey's actions demonstrated that he, and not his boss, was his toughest taskmaster.

In one obsessive patient after another, I've seen a similar pattern. They complain about the amount of time their work consumes, and the unremitting pressure under which they live. They talk about their demanding bosses, their need for financial security, the pressure to provide their families with a comfortable lifestyle. But in fact, when I go through the schedules of such "overworked" patients, I invariably see areas in which they *could* change without impairing their efficiency. When I suggest specific cutbacks, however, I am usually bombarded with justifications for every single commitment. The bottom line for the denying workaholic is that he cannot cut out anything. Or so he insists.

The Hidden Workaholic

Many obsessives are also "driven" in their spare time. They often feel compelled to use *all* their time productively. They're usually armed with lists of "things to do," and they're much more apt to fret about the items left undone than to savor the accomplishment of those they've checked off. They shudder at the thought of wasting time. Even in their "free" time, they feel they should be working on chores, projects, or other productive or educational tasks.

"I never relax," Therese told me unhappily. "There's always something to do. I either have to clean the house, pay bills, or something. And if I do take time off, I start to feel like I'm neglecting something. I feel lazy, and in my mind that's reprehensible."

At this point, I interrupted Therese to comment on how oddly that struck me, given how much she accomplishes in both her professional life and personally. Still, she demurred.

"I constantly feel I'm not doing everything I could be doing. I should be doing so much more reading. I should stay in better touch with friends and my family. I think forty percent of my time is spent feeling guilty. Even as I'm accomplishing things, I'm thinking about all I'm *not* getting done. I live with this sense that things need to be done every minute of the hour. And every minute that I'm not doing something, I feel disappointed in myself."

Although Therese worked only a "normal forty-hour" week, I would call her a "hidden workaholic." A similar drive to be productive at all times can even be found in those who are not formally employed. Claire, for instance, is a forty-eight-year-old homemaker who seems to be in constant motion. Every day she devotes many hours to housecleaning and maintenance, and she continues to practice such vanishing arts as baking pies, drying laundry on an outdoor clothesline, and raising herbs and flowers, which she then dries and mounts. As her three children grew up, Claire became more and more involved with community service organizations, and such volunteer work now consumes at least part of every day. While Claire will occasionally take a break to chat with one of her neighbors, she inevitably excuses herself to get back to her "messy house" or her long list of chores. Her brisk pace continues into each evening until she runs out of hours and reluctantly leaves tasks for the next day. She makes it sound as if she's always behind, and isn't quite measuring up to her own strict standards.

The Driving Forces

Every workaholic isn't necessarily obsessive. But most strongly obsessive people *are* workaholics—driven to overwork by any number of their obsessive traits, including the following leading culprits.

THE PRESSURE OF PERFECTIONISM

The person who can't tolerate making mistakes, or who has to be perceived as irreproachable, is more likely to find himself at his desk late at night, laboring to catch any possible error and striving to make his work perfect. Lydia, for example, was a thirty-one-year-old travel agent who worked until eight or nine o'clock every evening—two or three hours longer than all the other agents in her office. She was not paid for putting in the extra hours, but she couldn't bear the thought of overlooking any of the details that would give her clients the best possible trips. Whereas the other agents sometimes "wouldn't have time" to obtain seat assignments for their clients, for example, Lydia always got her people the very best seats possible. She also devoted hours to checking for the lowest fares.

"I really enjoy my time off," Lydia insisted. "And my husband has pleaded with me for years to come home earlier. I'd like to, but I really empathize with my clients, and I simply have to do my best for them."

Like Lydia, many of my obsessive clients seem to take conscientiousness—an otherwise laudable trait—to unnatural levels. "Sometimes I don't feel right at the end of the workday because I didn't give my employer his money's worth," an accountant named Frank told me. "I grew up in a family that believed if you didn't do a full day's work, you shouldn't take the money." Yet by any objective standard, Frank *always* took his work extremely seriously. He willingly accepted every task assigned to him, and never once dreamed of calling in sick or leaving early. To him a full day's work meant spending every second between 8:30 A.M. and 4:30 P.M. in the most productive way possible. He felt guilty on days when he "didn't accomplish enough," according to that standard. And yet it never occurred to him that on most days he gave his employer *more* than his money's worth.

One other aspect of perfectionism also can foster workaholism. Remember that subscribing to the Perfectionist's Credo often results in unproductive and time-consuming behavior patterns. Fear of making an error may cause the perfectionist to procrastinate, for instance, or he may waffle over decisions, or be unable to wrap up his projects. As a result, some perfectionists have to work longer just to accomplish the same amount as someone less perfectionistic.

THE ANGST OF ALL-OR-NOTHING

The familiar force of all-or-nothing thinking also shapes the work-heavy lifestyles of many obsessives. They seem to feel as if cutting back on their work hours even slightly will lead them to cut back more and ever more, eventually bringing them to a horrifying state of indolence.

Many find it hard to start certain projects, knowing that once they start they'll have trouble stopping before the task is completed (and perfectly, at that). Their reluctance to interrupt the work, in turn, comes partly from their knowledge that if they lose their momentum it will be hard to start up again. It's a vicious cycle that is conveyed by one character in Thomas Wolfe's *You Can't Go Home Again:*

> *"I've got an idea that a lot of the work in this world gets done by lazy people. That's the reason they work—because they're so lazy. . . . It's this way: You work because you're afraid not to. You work because you have to drive yourself to such a fury to begin. That part's just plain hell! It's so hard to get started that once you do you're afraid of slipping back. You'd rather do anything than go through that agony again—so you keep going . . . till you couldn't stop even if you wanted to. . . . Then people*

say you're a glutton for work, but it isn't so. It's laziness—just plain, damned, simple laziness, that's all."

WORK AS PROTECTION

Work can also serve to buffer the obsessive from things he or she would rather avoid. For instance, work makes for an admirable barrier to intimacy.

Leo, a radio announcer, insisted to his wife, Robin, that he accepted so many professional commitments because they needed the money. In fact, their arguments over financial matters were tainting their genuine affection for each other, destroying their sexual relationship, and causing both to be depressed. When they finally consulted me, Robin charged that Leo's busy schedule conveniently enabled him to avoid her. "I guess that might be true," Leo finally admitted after a few attempts at rationalization. "But can you blame me? Who would want to face all the pain and hostility that's built up between us?"

Another patient, Evelyn, was an extremely conscientious teacher who complained bitterly about her loneliness. She blamed her job for the fact that she was single and had virtually no social life; she put in phenomenally long hours both in the classroom and at home in the evenings and on weekends. While Evelyn said she hated this grind, she was passionately devoted to her students and couldn't imagine doing less for them. She felt she was only giving them what they needed and deserved, and she couldn't understand how other teachers could work less in good conscience.

One day another group member happened to question Evelyn's work patterns. Was it possible that Evelyn actually *feared* intimacy, and that to avoid even the possibility of such an involvement, she had barricaded herself behind her work? At this, Evelyn burst into tears and gasped, "I can't *believe* you would say such a thing! If only you knew how badly I want to be in a relationship." She was hurt beyond belief, and could not acknowledge, then or later, that there might be any truth to the suggestion. Yet the question had hit a nerve. Being an altruistic, ultra-dedicated teacher was so crucial to her pride and sense of self-worth that she couldn't bear any hint that her motives might be mixed—that is, that her workaholism might be a self-serving defense mechanism as well as arising from a desire to serve others.

A second way in which his work can protect the workaholic is by providing him with a noble excuse for avoiding various personal demands—demands with which he otherwise might feel duty-bound to comply. "It was much more fun to be a big shot downtown than to go home and change diapers," admitted one banker who reformed his hard-driving ways after suffering a massive heart attack. When Lenore, a workaholic attorney, followed her doctor's orders and took a week of vacation, she purposely didn't tell her parents. "I knew that they would want me to spend a lot of time with them if they knew I was free."

Immersion in work also can protect one from awareness of one's emotions. "I always overworked," Belinda, a research chemist, told me. "But when my husband died a few years ago, then I really became obsessive about it. I had no reason to go home. I see now that I was using work to mask my feelings and to keep myself at bay."

Still one more "protective" quality that the obsessive may find in work is a superstitious one. On some level he may feel that his diligence is racking up countless points with the Cosmic Scorekeeper. By putting in all those long hours, he denies himself pleasure for the present—but can expect to be rewarded someday, somehow, for his self-sacrifice.

Some people can't spend money on themselves without going through elaborate mental gyrations about whether they've earned the self-indulgence. "I owe it to myself," they'll state when telling me about some personal expenditure, adding pointedly, "I've worked so hard."

THE DRIVE OF DEMAND-SENSITIVITY, THINKAHOLISM, AND ORDERLINESS

As I discussed in chapter 5, obsessives tend to be acutely sensitive to both explicit and unspoken obligations. This heightened sensitivity can make one's work load heavier than that of a less demand-sensitive person. For example, when Mona's boss began working weekends, Mona felt compelled to join him in the office for at least a few hours. "He never once asked me to come in," she said. "But somehow I got the feeling that he really did think I should help out."

Thinkaholism can exert a different kind of pressure on these already overburdened individuals. Work provides rich fodder for the obsessive's tendency to dwell on problems. At the end of the day or the end of the week, many workaholics find it hard to shift their thoughts and attention away from their jobs, and as a result they may be preoccupied and "not fully present" with loved ones or in leisure activities.

Yet another contributor to workaholism can be the obsessive's need for orderliness. Work organizes one's time; it imposes an order upon existence. I can't count the number of obsessives who have told me that while work is hard, they prefer it to the uncertainty of unstructured time. At least, when they have tasks laid out before them, they can enjoy a sense of movement and virtuous productivity as they dispatch them. Orderliness also may increase their work load if it drives them to spend a lot of time on such activities as cleaning, organizing, and straightening their desks. Or they may feel compelled to stay late, until all the "loose ends" have been attended to.

WORK AS A MEANS OF CONTROL

Finally, many people see hard work as one of the most important tools for controlling their destinies, either indirectly, via the Scorekeeper (as

I've already mentioned), or directly. Since many obsessives never feel financially or professionally secure enough, no matter how much money they have, or how impressive their accomplishments, they may feel unable ever to turn down any opportunity to work more. Or they may be afraid to take time off work because of the attendant loss of control over everything from in-house politics to ensuring that things are done "their way."

"Control—or the illusion thereof—is vitally important to workaholics," writes researcher Marilyn Machlowitz. "The quest to achieve control is not simply a contest but a brutal, futile battle. Workaholics' cluttered calendars represent an attempt to 'beat the clock.' Their lists [of things to do] are but 'a way to organize the unorganizable.' . . . The perceived need for organization creates a tendency to cram all objectives into a stable, predictable, and inadequate amount of time in order to achieve a semblance of control."

Are You Too Driven?

If you spend practically every waking hour working—on either job-related tasks or other types of productive activities—you may be a workaholic. But what if you are? How driven is "too driven"?

To answer that question, try applying the same standard that many health professionals use for assessing alcohol consumption: Is the amount that you're working (or thinking about work) causing potentially serious problems in your life?

Once again, you need to consider costs versus benefits, but this is *unusually* difficult. Workaholism ranks among the most acceptable of all addictions; our society both reveres and rewards industriousness. That in itself can be one of the benefits of workaholism, but it also makes it easier to overlook or discount the costs of overwork. Sylvia, a fifty-seven-year-old businesswoman, once spent twenty minutes complaining to me about her crushing work load, but then added, "It's so easy to think of it all as a positive thing. Even as I'm telling you about my schedule, I'm feeling virtuous."

The Joy of Work

Work can be one of life's greatest pleasures. It provides many adults with their primary source of intellectual stimulation and social interaction. It may well be the only forum in which they can compete and win applause for their performance. Besides prestige, hard work often results in financial security, power, and career advancement.

Excitement is another dividend of a frantic schedule. You don't have to be the Secretary of State, jetting around the globe in pursuit of peace, in order to enjoy a work-induced adrenaline high. "It's literally like taking a drug," says Carl Thoresen, a Stanford University professor of education and psychology who has studied workaholics. "It's a euphoric, almost giddy feeling, such as you might have when you've just given a presentation. You feel terrific."

Many workaholics also find spiritual satisfaction in their work. Candace, a hard-driving art dealer, enjoys the money that her success has brought her, but she also sees her long hours as helping to launch new careers. "I feel like I'm making my own small contribution to the art world," she says. In similar fashion, engineers may be inspired by the thought of improving people's lives with the bridges they design, or hairdressers by their clients' pleasure in looking stylish.

The Costs of Workaholism

All these are very real benefits—but they're benefits of *work* rather than of workaholism, and they all can be enjoyed even if work plays a more balanced role in your life. Workaholism, too, may have its payoffs, but they often are far outweighed by the noxious consequences of giving work an overwhelming importance.

THE POISONING OF PERSONAL RELATIONSHIPS

First, workaholism sabotages your relationships, and for obvious reasons. There are a limited number of hours in the day, and if you fill them with work or thoughts of work, you can't have much time left for your family. Some workaholics avoid marriage for that reason, and it's common for women workaholics to postpone or reject childbearing altogether.

Shortchanged Children

If you do have children, you're likely to tell yourself that you're working as hard as you are for their sake—a sacrifice they may find of questionable value. In their book *The Addictive Organization,* Anne Wilson Schaef and Diane Fassel recount the words of one grown daughter of a workaholic:

> *Everything revolved around my father's work. If we got too playful and made noise we would be quieted because Daddy was either working or sleeping. When work went poorly, he was moody, angry, and destructive. When it went well, he was jolly. . . . We rarely saw him. Sometimes he stayed in the city overnight or on big projects, he would be gone for weeks at a time. . . . I don't think my mother or our family were ever second place in my father's life, I believe for him we didn't exist at all. I grew up spending an inordinate amount of time thinking about my father, yet never really knowing him. I hate him for this and I miss him deeply.*

As this woman's comments reveal, a workaholic parent may be physically present but nonexistent as a nurturing presence. Some work addicts experience their children's attempts at contact as annoying interruptions. Imagine what effect this must have upon the children's self-image.

Other workaholic parents may transform time spent together into time *working* together. Say it's a Sunday afternoon, and the parent has no pressing obligations; he really could afford to spend a few hours doing what his child most wants to do, say, playing ball. But because of the parent's chronic inner need to be accomplishing something, he hankers to be gardening, or repairing the back fence. So he tries to accomplish two things simultaneously—to spend time with his child and to work on the project—by cajoling the child into working with him.

If the project truly engages the child's interest, it may turn out to be a pleasant shared experience. But if the child senses that the parent is more involved in the fence than in him, the child will resent it. The parent may even compound the damage by acting disappointed by the child's lack of enthusiasm for the work, or critical of his or her contribution to it.

Some workaholic parents go one step further, getting annoyed whenever they find their children "wasting time." They want their children to share their own abhorrence for any hint of laziness, and they find tasks to fill the children's time—until the children get used to fleeing whenever they see the meddlesome parent approaching.

If work is keeping you from your children—either physically or emotionally—you may not realize what you're missing until it's too late. Many people see parenthood as an either/or proposition; they think you either have children or you don't. But in fact your children's childhoods are composed of hundreds of fleeting experiences: the first laughs of babyhood, the first steps, trick-or-treating at Halloween, high school courtships. Each stage of development lasts for only a very brief time, and, once completed, will never be repeated. Miss out on enough such experiences, and you will end up with only a pale, vitiated sense of ever having "had children."

Some people, realizing that this has happened, try to correct it too late. I've had several adult patients who received very little attention from their parents when they were children or adolescents. When the elderly parents (often newly widowed) finally sought companionship, the sons and daughters reacted with dread, shying away from contact and expressing such feelings as, "We have absolutely nothing in common," or "I don't feel any connection to him." Sometimes these adult children have expressed resentment at being approached after so many years of neglect. "Where was he when I needed him?" they ask.

Workaholism and Your Mate

As for your spouse, workaholism may not cause problems if you're both comfortable spending only limited time together. But when this is not the case, one partner's workaholism can make the other's life a lonely purgatory. Resentful, angry spouses also often find ways of retaliating—by withholding affection, undercutting their partner's standing with the children, having affairs, spending too much money, or otherwise making their discontent manifest. They may ultimately seek a divorce.

Even in the absence of such blatant discord, too much work is likely to take its toll on your sex life. Drs. William Masters and Virginia Johnson wrote: "There is little doubt that the intimate man-woman bond is profoundly affected . . . usually for worse, by conscious and/or unconscious feelings that are rooted in attitudes about work." The sex researchers cite "the kinds of husbands and wives who relentlessly search for new ways to occupy their time and use their energies— making more money, advancing in a career, caring for children, improving homes, doing community work, accumulating possessions—in short, doing anything that feels like work. . . . In that scheme of things, a sexual relationship has virtually no place. Coitus does because it is translated into a task, a chore, an obligation, a performance, something to be done."

Forgotten Friendships

Beyond one's immediate family, workaholism is apt to claim another important casualty: friendships. Again, that's because one of the most important elements in maintaining a rewarding friendship is frequent contact, with sufficient time together to talk about each other's lives, to relax and have fun together. Such contact can be as simple as taking a walk together. But if your free time collapses under the weight of work, your friendships will suffer.

Maintaining a happy family life and developing close friendships contribute immeasurably to one's fulfillment in life. But it's amazing how many workaholics fail to see time spent on relationships as productive. They may pay lip service to the importance of their relationships, and indeed often truly value them. But at the same time their behavior betrays the hidden conviction that it's somehow more important to put one's time and energy into work than into friends and family.

I think of Larry, a forty-year-old consultant, who came to me in part because his workaholism was threatening his marriage. He loved his wife very much, and seemed willing to try to make changes in his lifestyle. For example, he agreed to refrain from doing any work for one entire weekend. When I asked him how it went, he told me he'd been plagued by the feeling that he was wasting time, that he should have been accomplishing something.

"What did you do?" I asked.

"Victoria and I spent the whole weekend just playing together. We went sailing on Saturday and went for a long hike on Sunday. We really relaxed."

"But you just said you didn't get anything accomplished."

"I meant *work!*" he laughed.

One reason workaholics like Larry may see "fun weekends" (and other leisure activities) as being "wasted" time is that the good relationships, personal fulfillment, and increased self-awareness that spring from such time are not as concrete as the most common reward for long, hard work, namely money.

WORK AND COUNTERPRODUCTIVITY

Workaholism causes problems in more than just the personal realm. "Keeping one's nose to the grindstone can hurt . . . business," concluded *The Wall Street Journal* in an article about workaholic entrepreneurs. "The prolonged stress of fighting distraction, focusing intensely on dull details and working at protracted tasks fatigues the mind. . . . The result: a rise in errors, troubles handling the public, more accidents, and declining workmanship."

As previously noted, perfectionists often have trouble starting projects, making decisions, and delegating tasks that could be better executed by others—all of which may easily do more damage than the good done during all those extra hours on the job. At the same time, the perfectionist's constant fault-finding is apt to dampen office morale.

Even in the absence of such harmful behaviors, there still remains the question of whether the workaholic is putting all those hours to productive use. In one 1987 article on overwork, *Fortune* magazine described how a management consultant spent three days following one "hard-driving, bleary-eyed investment banker," recording in minute detail what the man did in the course of his interminable workdays. The consultant found that *eighty percent* of the Wall Streeter's activities turned out to be "busy work": redundant phone conversations, unnecessary meetings, time spent packing and unpacking his two bulging briefcases. All too often, no one looks at how *effectively* the workaholic is laboring, and yet that ultimately is much more important than the number of hours he spends on the job.

CHRONIC LEISURE-DEPRIVATION

By definition, workaholics don't have much free time, and chronic leisure-deprivation in itself may cause both psychological and physiological damage. Among the varied medical ailments attributed to overwork are fatigue, irritability, sleep disturbances, difficulty in concentrating, depression, gastrointestinal malfunctions, coronary disease, hypertension, headaches, and muscle spasms.

Even those maladies pale when compared to the bleak sense of desperation and suffering that can overtake someone in the throes of burnout. Forty-seven-year-old Dave sounded as if his staggering work load had crushed all the enthusiasm out of him. A successful psychologist, he generally saw clients all day long, often well into the evening, and he fielded telephone calls at other odd hours. In addition, Dave also lectured two or three times a week. Nights and weekends, he labored away on his third book. He saw no way to extricate himself from any of these commitments, and with an expensive house payment and three children in private schools, he also felt considerable financial pressure.

"Sometimes I just feel like the better part of my life is over. I used to live for my weekends and vacations. I really enjoyed them, but now all I do is work. I even find myself resenting my clients, the people who are depending on me to help them." Morosely, Dave confided that he was experiencing a kind of existential depression. Besides work, his thoughts were increasingly filled with ruminations on the sad and bleak aspects of life. "Sometimes I wonder what the point of it all is. I mean, is this as good as it gets? Do you just work all your life, get sick, and die?"

Of course, burnout afflicts both those who are forced by circumstances into overworking and those who are *psychologically* driven to work all the time. But of the two groups, overly driven obsessives are less likely to be able to enjoy whatever small amounts of leisure time they do have. I think of a letter to the editor of a local newspaper I read recently, in which the writer explained that he and his wife found it necessary, when planning vacations, to do the following: "After determining primary and alternative places we want to visit, we study all necessary maps and write out driving instructions for each day in detail, giving directions, route or highway number, and all other pertinent data including in-city directions. This enables us (1) to realize the deficiencies of maps before leaving (and maybe buy more to plan better), (2) synthesize instructions from several maps, (3) select the vital maps to take and (4) make driving decisions before being confronted with major problems on the road we might have foreseen and eliminated." Although this letter-writer claimed that "this preparation doesn't take much time," it is the type of "work" for which many obsessives trade away their leisure.

Other workaholics might cook elaborate dinners or take on complex home-improvement projects. Such laborious "play" can be truly pleasurable, but it's also very common for demand-sensitivity insidiously to drain the fun out of freely chosen leisure activities, making them feel like things that should or even must be done—in other words, like simply more work.

Furthermore, life holds a whole separate class of pleasures—things like basking in the sun or staying late in bed or sitting in a garden and listening to the birds sing—which many workaholics either completely miss out on or can't fully enjoy. When they take the time to dine with friends or go to a movie, they're apt to feel guilt or pressure to get back to something more productive. When I asked Vincent, a forty-year-old airline executive, how he felt while relaxing at home, his immediate response was that he felt fine. But then, as he thought about it, he added, "When I watch TV, I tend to feel guilty that I'm not getting one thing or another done. Or I'll watch for a few hours, and then afterward regret that I 'blew' the time and could have been doing something productive."

Caroline, the marketing director for a large clothing company, one day described her feelings about spending time with her baby and preschooler on the weekends.

"I love my children more than anything else in the world, and I don't have that much time with them during the week. Yet I find it very hard to spend completely unstructured time with them. Half the time I devise activities for us: we go somewhere or we undertake some project. About the only way I can force myself to just hang out with them and play spontaneously is by telling myself that it's my 'job' as a good mother to do that. And then it's okay. But it's sad that I can't fully surrender myself to their world."

If you're the kind of person who delights in being constantly on the go, you may be thinking that you can do very nicely, thank you, without ever sampling the joys of the couch potato. Just keep in mind that you may not be aware of what your hectic pace is costing you.

Danielle was a perfectionistic workaholic who used her vacations to travel extensively; once on the road, she was a relentless sightseer. If she wasn't out the door and heading for a museum by nine in the morning, she became tense; should a vacation end before she had hit all the "things to see" in her guidebooks, she felt cheated and unhappy. These underlying tensions burst into full bloom when she started to travel with her boyfriend, Jack, who took the view that touring should be leavened with long mornings in bed and lazy breakfasts spent with coffee and local papers. According to Danielle, "We were both stubborn and we would kind of dig in our heels. He seemed to get slower and slower, or else he'd get sick. And I resented him more and more."

With the relationship on the rocks, Danielle finally took a trip to Paris alone. While there, she was joined by a longtime woman friend. "Gail is more like Jack; she likes to take it kind of easy. We got into a sort of routine where we'd get up and have coffee, do one thing, have lunch and wine, and then do one other thing in the afternoon. And I didn't feel the same sort of conflict I always felt with Jack, whom

I had come to think of as a wimp. I guess I was more objective about Gail, and to my surprise I found that I actually sort of *preferred* this schedule. I began to think, 'Maybe there *hasn't* been something wrong with Jack. Maybe it's wrong with me.' And I just started to enjoy relaxing and hanging out more. Since then, I've made the conscious decision that I don't have to see everything while traveling. I've learned to prioritize and try to see just the best."

Becoming Less Driven

As we've seen, workaholism is an extremely complex phenomenon that can be shaped by many factors. Consequently, there's no single path to change. Nonetheless, change is possible. As a starting point, ask yourself:

- Are those long hours *really* an unavoidable requirement of the job?

- When was the last time you took a walk, going nowhere special? Or sat and listened to music? Or window-shopped?

- Do your co-workers (or people in comparable positions elsewhere) put in as much time as you do, and if not, how do *they* avoid it?

- Could your own perfectionism be driving you, and is it really worth it?

- Are you avoiding being home, for any reason?

- If you've taken on extra part-time work, is it because you really need the extra money? Or is a craving for absolutely guaranteed financial security shaping your behavior?

■ If you're self-employed, must you really accept every referral or project, or are you distorting things? For instance, how true is it that if you don't accept that referral, you'll never get another one from that person or firm? Even if that *did* happen, would it really endanger your security?

■ As for being preoccupied with work during your "free" time, how necessary or useful is this, really? How often do you *actually* get a creative idea or solve a work problem when you're with your family or engaged in leisure-time activities? Isn't it more likely that "thinkaholism" is contaminating your leisure?

A TWO-MONTH LEISURE-RECLAMATION PROGRAM

If work has taken over your life, are you willing to try an experiment? For a limited period, can you spend less time working and more time living? To achieve that goal, I suggest you make the following changes for two months. (Don't tell me. You're thinking, "I'll lose my job!" But how likely is that, really? And even if you did, would that be so dreadful—if workaholism is destroying your family life and/or harming your health?) At the end of the two months, evaluate the impact on your life. If you find you're not significantly happier, you can always go back to the way you were.

1. Separate your work from home life. Don't take work home with you. Or, if your job requires you to do all or part of your work at home, confine it to one room, preferably one that you can close off and leave behind.

2. Limit your work sessions, and when the appointed quitting time comes, stop working, even if you're not completely finished. I'm not suggesting you be irresponsible and leave crucial

tasks for the next day. But too many obsessives tell themselves that *everything* is crucial. Don't sit there at your desk, doing one last thing, and yet one more, unless they really are imperative.

3. Don't work weekends, unless doing so is absolutely critical. If it is, be miserly in the amount of time you give up. Remember the words of the Chinese writer/philosopher Lin Yutang, "Those who are wise won't be busy, and those who are too busy can't be wise. The wisest man is therefore he who loafs most gracefully." According to Lin, there are "three great American vices": efficiency, punctuality, and the desire for achievement and success. These "are the things that make the Americans so unhappy and so nervous. They steal from them their inalienable right of loafing and cheat them of many a good, idle and beautiful afternoon."

4. Whenever it's time to stop working, consciously shift your mental focus to enjoying your free time. It may help to mark the transition from work to "play" in some way, by taking several deep breaths, for instance, or doing some stretching when you finally stand up and step away from your desk at the close of your work day.

Once you've left, concentrate on relaxing and thinking pleasant thoughts about loved ones or home. If you begin to feel uncomfortable or guilty about "not accomplishing anything," fight those feelings. Ask: "What is so terrible about taking the time to read this book, or enjoy this conversation? Don't I deserve to enjoy life just as much as anybody else?"

5. Any time you slip into ruminations or worries about work, do the thought-stopping exercise: slap your thigh or blink,

breathe deeply, tell yourself, "That's not helping," and refocus your thoughts.

6. Strictly limit the time you spend on chores. Before tackling any project, ask, "Is this really so important? Do I want to spend most of my 'off' time for the rest of my life worrying about things like this? And if not, why not start to change that now?"

You may need to remind yourself that you're not showing defective character when you take the time to enjoy yourself when items on your list remain undone. As with professional tasks, the list of personal tasks you "need to do" will never end, so don't have that as your goal. It's unreasonable to refuse to enjoy yourself just because you have unfinished chores, since you'll have them for the rest of your life.

It's possible that you're devoting a great deal of time and mental energy to things that, in the big picture, are not terribly significant. To me, chores and errands are maintenance, similar to having the oil changed in your car. The whole reason for maintenance is to keep the vehicle running. Maintenance shouldn't be an end in itself, but a means to more enjoyable and effective living. Obsessives tend to get caught up with maintenance, at the expense of really living. They spend extra time ordering, fixing, straightening, tending to small details, as life speeds by. One patient said, "I seem to spend most of my time doing mindless busy work, but I don't seem to be living. I don't feel like I'm really living."

7. If you have an opportunity to refuse extra work, do so, if only during this two-month period. If that idea frightens you, this is one of those rare situations where I would advise you to sit down with a friend, spouse, or trusted colleague and use that

person as a sounding board. Describe your fears, and ask how realistic they are. It's amazing how distorted your sense of your own worth can be. An objective viewpoint may help you see that it's ridiculous to think no one will ever refer a case to you again if you turn one down. Other people certainly must recognize your value, and they'll refer to you as soon as you're "open for business" again.

The same advice applies if you're tempted to decline a promotion because you're already working too hard. Obsessives typically pride themselves on their capacity to do enormous amounts of work, and they sometimes forget that they are also valued for other qualities. They may fear their employer would question their dedication if they sacrificed themselves less. Too insecure to set limits, they wind up overworking.

Again, I recommend that you talk to a colleague to see if such perceptions are accurate. Would it really be dangerous not to jump so willingly to take on increasingly more work, or even to beg off occasionally? Isn't it reasonable to be able to say *occasionally*, "I'm sorry, but I'm just swamped right now and can't take that on at the moment"? Chances are good that you're much more important to your employer than you realize.

8. During activities with family or friends, *be in the moment,* even if you have left work to be done. Don't let yourself think of your spouse or children as nuisances that are keeping you from more important things. Take an active interest in their conversation. Really listen to what they are saying, instead of tuning them out to ruminate about work-related problems.

Living in the present moment is one of the most difficult challenges imaginable for many obsessives, and this is exactly what I'm asking you to do more of. Practice is the golden key to achieving this. It takes time to change, so start now. Now is the time to experience your family and friends, to enjoy time off, to pursue your leisure-time interests. Now is the time to enjoy life. Remember, *none of us can know for certain that we have any time other than the present moment.*

As you put the above suggestions into practice, expect resistance to come from both within and without. "Workaholism is the most socially acceptable of the addictions because it is so socially productive," write Schaef and Fassel. "Many people have responded to our description of workaholism with statements like, 'It is not the same as alcoholics, who destroy themselves and their loved ones; workaholics are productive members of the society.' We have to realize that for some organizations and for some people, destroying one's life and loved ones is acceptable if one produces something useful in the society."

If you think the steps I have described might help you, don't put off starting them! More than one patient has said, "You're right. All this work is ruining my life. And I'm going to do something about it—next month." Or "as soon as I finish this assignment." Or "just as soon as I can get my nest egg together."

Many people toil for years to achieve a "comfortable" future, only to wind up with a few years of retirement in which either they or their spouses are in poor health. They get to do only a fraction of the things they had looked forward to doing, and they feel bitter disappointment.

Finding the appropriate balance between work and the rest of your life may never be easy for you. But it's imperative to try. I like to remember the man who remarked that he had never heard of anyone on his deathbed saying, "My only regret is that I didn't work more." You too are unlikely to die with such a regret. But if work dominates your life, will you be left with other, worse forms of remorse—over children that you never really knew, or intimate bonds that you sacrificed on the altar of overtime, a lifetime full of roses that you never stopped to smell?

T E N

Living with
the Obsessive

There is no good in arguing with the inevitable. The only argument available with an east wind is to put on your overcoat.
—JAMES RUSSELL LOWELL,
Democracy and Other Addresses

L ife with an obsessive can be challenging. Although I've mostly been describing how their behavior causes *them* to suffer, it can be equally painful to be on the receiving end of such traits as the following:

Pickiness: You feel as if you can never do anything right. You may begin to wonder if the critical obsessive likes anything about you.

Demand-resistance: You often can't obtain the simple cooperation that oils the wheels of daily living.

Guardedness: You may never feel as if you really know the obsessive, or achieve a sense of intimacy with him. In the face of his or her aloofness, you may (mistakenly) feel unloved.

Rigidity: You can never count on obsessives to accept even minor changes. Instead, they're likely to be annoyed whenever you do something a little differently. And once they make up their mind about something, it's practically impossible to persuade them to change it.

Excessive orderliness: You may be made to feel guilty if you don't share the same level of orderliness. If they insist that you meet their standards for neatness, this may put you under a lot of pressure, creating resentment on your part, or a sense of oppression.

Infallibility: You can never win an argument with an obsessive, or point out any errors. So you may chronically get the message that you're wrong.

Workaholism: You may resent how little time and energy the other person devotes to your relationship. His or her chronic absence or preoccupation may make you feel unimportant.

Indecisiveness or inability to commit: You may be unable to make plans because of his or her waffling; you may be unsure where your relationship stands.

If you have an obsessive spouse, friend, co-worker, or relative, you may have only one of these complaints or all of them, or you may have others I haven't listed. Because obsessiveness can contribute to such a wide spectrum of interpersonal problems, it's impossible to spell out ways for dealing with every one of them. Instead, I offer seven broad suggestions for getting along more smoothly with the too-perfect people in your life.

1. Don't Take Their Foibles Personally

Obsessive behavior usually stems from deep-seated fears, and not from any malice toward you. Yet it's easy to lose sight of this. If hardly a day passes without your spouse criticizing something you do, you may feel as if he or she regards you in a fairly dim light. Worse, you may start seeing yourself that way.

Try to remember that your mate's finely tuned sensors would find fault with even the saintliest, most infallible person. If an obsessive friend always seems to be busy when *you* call *her,* don't assume she's trying to avoid you. Having to be the one who initiates contacts between you may reflect her need to feel in control of the relationship.

If another friend consistently balks at your suggestions, you may feel that he's ignoring your feelings, or considers you unintelligent. It's more likely that, at some level, he fears being influenced or controlled, not just by you, but by anyone, and that resisting reassures him that he can have an impact on the forces around him (such as you).

Remember that the obsessive's personality was formed long before he met you, and he would demonstrate this behavior with anyone—especially someone important to him. This understanding can make the obsessive's comments or actions less hurtful.

2. Recognize That *They* May Be Taking *Your* Quirks Personally

When you resist doing things their way, some obsessives may interpret your lack of compliance as evidence that you don't care about them. And while their in-control, invulnerable personas usually won't allow them to admit how much it hurts them to feel unloved in this way, the hurt feelings may be simmering just below the surface, and they may profoundly affect your interactions.

Hank, a forty-five-year-old engineer, and his wife, Sharon, both told me that one of their biggest problems sprang from Hank's terrible temper. "He doesn't seem to realize when he's being unreasonable," Sharon said. "When he comes home from work, he looks around for things that haven't been done. Then he explodes at the kids [two teenage boys] and me. We're on the defensive so much of the time."

A picture of the household quickly emerged. Sharon was a piano teacher who gave lessons to students in her home in addition to handling the housework. Hank worked long hours in a very demanding job in order to support his family's comfortable lifestyle and send his sons to good schools. He felt that all he asked in return was that they do "a few very easy things": attend to certain gardening tasks, for instance, or keep the contents of the silverware drawer straight. Hank saw these and a multitude of similar tasks as being self-evidently important, and he also went to some lengths to get the others to agree that they *needed* to be done; that if one of the knives was pointing the wrong way, for example, someone could get hurt. In fact, Sharon and the boys complained that Hank greatly belabored these points.

"He goes on and on," Sharon complained. "The kids will say, 'Okay, Dad. For God's sake! I understand!' But he won't let it drop."

Hank interrupted, "They *say* they'll do something, but obviously I'm not getting through to them, because when I get home it still isn't done. So the yelling and anger is necessary. It's the only thing that gets results."

But what "results" were his angry outbursts achieving? Sharon felt misunderstood and resentful, and the boys were tense and frustrated. Hank admitted that an atmosphere of uneasiness had invaded their home, and it pained him as much as it did the others that their love for one another was being eroded by their continual skirmishes.

I asked him how he *felt* when he came home to find tasks undone.

"I'm upset," he replied. "I feel like, damn it, I have to put up with so much garbage at work, and then at home she can't even do these little things for me. If I ask her to take care of three or four things that need to be done and she doesn't do them . . ."

"What does that mean to you?"

"It means she doesn't care enough about my feelings. . . . She doesn't put a high priority on what I want."

"So the bottom line is caring?"

"Yes, and that, unfortunately, you can only rely on yourself."

Sharon was shocked by these revelations. She did in fact care about Hank. She loved him, and worked hard both at teaching and tending house. She also felt that she and the boys did most of the things he asked of them, and that Hank only focused on the exceptions.

Hank and she also perceived the tasks themselves in completely different ways. Sharon *detested* weeding, for instance; to her, it felt like horrible drudgery and an incredible waste of her time, rather than the inconsequential task that Hank saw it to be. Though a reasonably neat person, she hardly even *saw* much of the disorder that was so upsetting to her ultra-fastidious husband. (And I could empathize with this. During his first visit with me, Hank confided that it was all he could do to restrain himself from going and untangling my messy telephone cord—a source of disorder to which I had been completely oblivious.)

It took a real effort for Sharon to see the world as Hank saw it, and the fact that she naturally tended to see it differently had nothing at all to do with whether or not she loved him.

I tried to help both Sharon and Hank become aware of how personally Hank was taking her failure and that of the boys to comply with all his requests. Every time Hank confronted those uncompleted tasks, he was suffused with disappointment; the people he cared most about in the world weren't taking him seriously. His wishes didn't matter to them, and meanwhile they were living off his labor. He felt exploited and unloved.

I also explained to Hank how radically Sharon's perceptions differed from his own, and how difficult it was for her to see certain things as he wished her to. I challenged Hank to reexamine some of his premises. Would the world really end if the yard wasn't free of weeds, or the silverware didn't all point in the same direction? I urged him to acknowledge that he was requesting certain things *because they were important to him,* and not because it was objectively imperative that they be done. And even if his demands were reasonable, I asked, was being right worth alienating his family?

As it turned out, both Hank and Sharon were able to make some changes. After twenty-three years of marriage, Hank finally began to understand that no matter how "right" he was about keeping things in order, all his arguments, lectures, rages, and logical "proofs" of the correctness of his positions *were actually counterproductive.* He acknowledged that not only were his demands not being met, but his family literally dreaded his presence. It finally struck home that no amount of logical argument could make Sharon experience the world exactly as he did, and that even when she and the boys yielded to his demands, they did so resentfully, and felt more alienated from him.

Seeing the *inefficacy* of his behavior enabled Hank to begin limiting his demands. He stopped the lectures and explanations altogether. In turn, Sharon started to do more for him, both out of affection and out of gratitude for his willingness to work on improving their family life. She knew how terribly difficult it was for him to change these ingrained behaviors, and as she saw him struggle with himself in a genuine, good-faith effort to change, she began to reconnect with her old feelings of love for him.

She also learned to avoid agreeing to do a task unless she was certain she really could and would do it, which brings us to:

3. Be Consistent and Trustworthy

It's tempting to feign agreement with some obsessives just to get them to stop badgering you. But this can backfire! Obsessives need to be able to feel they can trust you, either to say openly that you're *not* going to comply (giving your reasons), or actually to follow through on your word. Even in the smallest things, most obsessives respond dramatically to any evidence that they can't trust you. They immediately wonder what *other* things you've been dishonest about. Can they believe you when you say you love them? Can they *ever* believe you or trust that you'll do what you agree to do?

Most obsessives need a sense of certainty and predictability. One man stated, "I need consistency in my life—to the extent that that's possible. I feel it would be nice if I came home at night and found consistency there. If I'm told dinner will be at six-thirty and I get home to find it's not even started—"

"That only happened once!" his wife protested, but her husband continued on, undeterred.

"I anticipate that things will be a certain way, and I don't want to be surprised. I want to know what to expect."

Most obsessives prize candor and honesty more than other people do. Yet because many can't rest until you cry "uncle" and see the rightness of their position you may feel you're in a no-win situation: If you hold on to your point of view, you'll be accused of being impractical or illogical (and therefore unjustified in feeling the way you do). And if you give in, over your obvious objections, just to end the lecture or argument, you'll be perceived as dishonest and untrustworthy.

What can you do in that position?

4. Don't Be Pressured into Disavowing Your Own Feelings and Preferences

Even if you can't win a debate demonstrating the superiority of your position, *you still are entitled to your own view.* You should feel free to assert that right.

Unless you're equally obsessive, you're probably no match for an obsessive in a logical argument. Obsessives spend their lives analyzing things; they're experts at it. But just because a course of action seems to be more efficient, practical, or logical to him or her, you still don't have to choose it. Don't be shamed or bullied into doing so. Practicality is only *one* criterion of worthiness. *Other criteria are just as important,* such as likes, dislikes, pleasure, and personal values. You have every right to your own preferences and your own way of doing things unless your behavior is clearly and significantly irresponsible or damaging. By the same token, when someone else is interfering with *your* enjoyment of life, you have the right to object, even if you can't prove, logically, that their behavior is "wrong."

There's nothing wrong with having different notions of what's important and what's trivial. If you agree to do some things another person's way, realize that it's not necessarily because you have adopted his values and your way is inferior, but that you are doing it because you care for the other person, because of his *anxieties* about disorder, chaos, lack of control. If something truly conflicts with your values (e.g., a disagreement about how to handle your children, or some other important matter), listen to his argument and think it over when you're alone. Then figure out what your position is, and reopen the discussion. Don't give in just to silence him or her. Don't be afraid to ask for time to think it over.

5. Don't Pressure the Obsessive

What about when *you* want the obsessive to do something—anything from making a simple decision to changing some deeply entrenched pattern?

Be forewarned: any direct confrontation in which you try to force the other person to change is almost certainly doomed to failure. Your request or demand will only increase his inclination to assert his dominance or "rightness," escalating the power struggle.

I'm reminded of an interaction that a patient related to me. He and a fellow lawyer were choosing between two available offices in a building they planned to share. Hal, my patient, was perfectly content to give his associate first choice, but the other man was vacillating, holding up Hal's move into the new quarters. Hal related one of their conversations:

"Once again, I asked him which one he wanted, and he told me he still couldn't decide. Since he'd been leaning toward number two, I told him that he could have it and I would take the other one. But he hit the roof, telling me that he hadn't said he wanted number two, and that the rent was higher. So I said, 'Okay. You take number one and I'll take number two.'

" 'Number one is too small.'

" 'Would you rather I chose?'

" 'No! I was here first, so I think I deserve first choice.'

" 'Do you have any idea when you'll know which office you want?'

" 'I don't know.' "

At first, maybe the other man's goal really was, as he consciously believed, simply to pick the office that best suited his needs; secondarily he may have enjoyed the sense of control he felt in making Hal wait. But when Hal pressured him, that changed. The associate became more invested in keeping the control, which he did by obstructing Hal.

The more impatient Hal got, the more determined the other was to delay his decision, because by now he was angry. He couldn't show it directly because he had no logical reason for it. So instead he unconsciously retaliated by blocking Hal.

I suggested that Hal try backing off completely—that he tell the associate to take his time and call whenever he had decided. When I saw Hal a week later, he said that when given that leeway, his associate had decided instantly.

The moral: Don't try to force the obsessive to do anything. You almost certainly won't succeed. More than other people, obsessives tend to resist pressure with an astonishing obstinacy. Even subtle pressure will likely fail, given the obsessive's keen ability to sense and chafe at even the most veiled demands. (And should he yield, you might pay a heavy price in the form of his resentment against you for pressuring him.)

At the same time, I'm not saying you should silently tolerate your obsessive friend's every quirk, no matter how outrageous. If a particular behavior is intolerable, tell him clearly and frankly how you feel, at the same time being sensitive as to how you present your message. Instead of saying, "You must change," for example, make sure you're conveying, "I would like you to do this, for reasons x, y, and z." If you have to know your boss's plans by a certain date, tell him so, but be sure to explain why, so that he doesn't interpret your need to know as an ultimatum, a control play, or manipulation. Your reasons should always reflect *your own needs, or your difficulty with the status quo,* rather than a *judgment* about the obsessive's behavior. For instance, say, "If I don't find out your plans by such-and-such a time, I won't be able to obtain a reduced rate ticket," *not,* "I hate it when you do this to me. You always make me wait, and it's so inconsiderate!"

Yet another alternative is to look for ways to solve your problem that don't require the obsessive person to alter his ingrained behavior patterns. Say, for example, that your spouse is chronically late when you're supposed to go somewhere together, and that this is a source of friction and tension between you. The more you nag and badger him, the more he drags his heels. If, after you try explaining why you so dislike being late, you still see no substantial change, you might consider other possible solutions, such as diplomatically making contingency plans for going places separately.

In any case, avoid a blaming posture; it simply won't help. Concentrate on coming up with a solution that you can really live with, indefinitely. Forget about who is right. Focus on the fact that *you* simply want to act in a way that makes you feel good, which means being on time, and try to come up with a solution that's fairly comfortable, if not optimal for both of you.

While change in the obsessive must come from within, sometimes healthy, truly unilateral changes in one partner will inspire change in the other. We aren't sure why this happens, but some would say that one person's chronic tardiness and its outcome—the partner's nagging and pushing him—is a re-creation of some aspect of a childhood relationship, and that it suits some need in each party. This view says that when one refuses to continue in the role of nagging, disappointed, disapproving parent, the other loses his unwitting collaborator and drops the corresponding role.

6. Foster Your Own Self-Esteem and Independence

Many obsessives hate to be dependent upon anything or anyone; they equate dependency with vulnerability. Unconsciously they feel that allowing their lives to revolve around another person would leave them open to utter devastation—should the other person turn against them, for example, or stop loving them, or even die. As a result, most don't let themselves depend too heavily upon even their closest friends and lovers.

I think that the friends and lovers of obsessives would do well to follow suit.

It's not that obsessives are in any sense undependable. On the contrary, their conscientiousness and consistency usually make them more reliable than other people. But at the same time, if you cling too much to your obsessive friend or lover, your very neediness may wind up making him anxious and repelling him.

For one thing, if you've made yourself completely dependent upon him, the obsessive may feel that you've imposed on him the frightening or burdensome responsibility of being absolutely indispensable to your emotional well-being. Given his need for a sense of options and freedom, this may both frighten and anger him. Love can't possibly survive in this climate.

Obsessives are also likely to see independence not just as something they prefer for themselves, but as an objective virtue. If they perceive you as needy and dependent, they may lose respect for you, or interest in you.

Another aspect of being emotionally dependent on a relationship is that your sense of worth often comes to rely upon feedback from the other person. Even minor variations in that feedback may cause your self-esteem and sense of security to plunge or soar. You're really setting yourself up for emotional turbulence if you rely too heavily upon approval or praise from some obsessives, because they aren't particularly good at expressing these things. Remember: their style of perception is to notice and be bothered by what's *not* right with things. And their need to guard their emotions may make it hard for them to show positive feelings or appreciation.

If you sense that your dependency upon an obsessive friend or lover may be harming you or the relationship, you can take some steps toward change. Start by trying to rediscover who *you* are—who you were before you met the other person. Work on developing separate interests and then pursue them vigorously, just as you would have if you had not become involved at this time. Strive to become a whole person, independent of any relationship.

As you struggle to establish your separate self, feelings of anxiety and insecurity may assail you. You may feel empty or isolated at first. You may worry that you are jeopardizing the relationship by not paying it enough attention. Fight these feelings! Try to act as if you felt strong and safe. Don't let the other person get the idea that your happiness or security depends entirely upon reassurance from him or her. More important, don't *you* accept that notion as unalterably true, because it isn't.

What *is* true is that at some point your friend or lover *could* decide to end the relationship, and you have no control over that. Throughout this book, I've discussed self-defeating aspects of the obsessive's need for complete control. The same dynamic applies to you. The more you attempt to mold your relationship, the more vigilantly you watch over it, the more likely you are to poison it. In some respects, the commitment-fearing obsessive is like a cat: most likely to remain close to you when you're absorbed in your own interests and to scoot away when you embrace it too vigorously.

Learn to accept the fact that any relationship could end. Find a way to resign yourself to that possibility. It's true that it would be extremely painful, but in the vast majority of cases, that pain is temporary. Don't think for a moment that you couldn't get through it. You could. And, just as you have before, you would eventually find happiness with someone else.

7. Reinforce Positive Changes— But Do It Sensitively

I've stressed how hard it is for obsessives to change. But many nonetheless manage to do so. If your spouse, parent, co-worker, or friend does begin to behave less obsessively, you need to realize that this is a real accomplishment that shows not only strength and courage, but a commitment to making your relationship better. Often it's an act of love.

The other person will almost certainly appreciate your understanding that it wasn't easy. But be careful how you demonstrate your approval.

Drawing attention to changes in the obsessive may make him uneasy. For one thing, he may still feel tentative about the changes, and too blatant an acknowledgment of them may make him feel more committed to maintaining them than he can tolerate.

You also must consider the impact of the obsessive's all-or-nothing thinking. If you react too strongly to the slightest improvement (if, for example, he comes home from work an hour earlier than usual), he may fear that you'll expect him to do it every night. If you comment favorably on his decreased demands for orderliness, again his anxiety might rise. He may think that now you'll expect him to change still *more,* and he may dig in his heels. Similarly, if you overreact to signs that he may be moving closer to making a commitment to you, he may fear that he's getting your hopes up too high. Most obsessives can't stand to break their word or fall short of expectations, and they dread the thought of hearing later, "But why did you lead me on?" This fear, combined with a dread of losing options, has stopped many obsessives cold.

You'll probably do better to reinforce behavioral improvements in only the most subtle, gentle ways. Effective reinforcers vary from one person to another. Most people like such things as affection, praise, or sex, but not everyone. Some respond best to silence, food, or even distance. You have to tune in to *your* obsessive and discern his or her specific reinforcers.

Barbara was able to do this. She first called me and made an appointment for couples therapy, but when the time came, her lover, David, changed his mind and refused to come with her. I had always felt that the only proper way to do couples therapy was to see both people together, so I expressed doubts about continuing. But Barbara implored me to try working with her alone, and I'm glad I did.

Tall and effervescent, Barbara had quickly fallen in love with David, a successful entrepreneur. She had thought that they would eventually marry and have children, but now found herself wondering whether David would ever be ready to commit himself. After a year and a half, the relationship didn't seem to be progressing; in fact, she and David were increasingly finding themselves at odds over Barbara's need for frequent reassurance of his love. On the nights David chose to sleep at home instead of at her place, she wondered if he was feeling alienated from her. When she would call and ask, he felt badgered and annoyed.

Since direct questions about his level of commitment irritated David, Barbara tried to assess it more covertly. At one point, for example, she wondered aloud to David whether he would like her to plan her vacation for the same two weeks as his. (Her implied question: "Are you willing to spend that time together?") David told her, some-what curtly, to plan her vacation for "whenever you want." (His unstated answer: "I'm not sure how I feel, so I don't want to commit myself to spending that time with you. I may or may not want to, and I won't know until the time comes. If I decide not to, I don't want to feel guilty for disappointing you.")

At the outset, I presented Barbara with the grim prospect that David might not change much, no matter what she did, but she remained determined. She saw so much good in the relationship that she couldn't bear to let it go without a fight. She thus set two main goals: to help David feel more comfortable about committing himself, and to promote more intimacy and affection between them.

One of the first things she did was to revise her view of David's very real fear of committing himself to *any* relationship. It was slow and difficult at first, but eventually Barbara began to accept the fact that his hesitancy did not reflect any personal rejection of her. Only then was she able to consider ways to reassure him that he was still a free man, with the option to change his mind at any time.

For one thing, she identified some of her own behaviors that were pushing David away—pouncing gleefully upon any signs that he was leaning toward a stronger commitment, for instance. Instead, Barbara learned to make little or no fuss when he showed signs of moving closer to her. In fact, she would redouble her efforts to maintain her own separate interests (as hard as that was for her initially).

Barbara also learned to temper her resentment of David's friend Brett, whom she had seen as competing for David's time and attention. During therapy, she came to realize that neither David's friendship with Brett nor any of his other separate interests truly threatened his relationship with her. What did threaten it was her own insecurity, which led her to *view* these things as threats, to complain about them, and to seek repeated assurances about David's level of commitment.

This insight eventually enabled her to begin to reshape her attitude toward Brett. Not only did she stop complaining, but she stopped resenting him. In fact, she began to see positive aspects of the friendship and was able to express these thoughts to David. At this point she stumbled upon an observation that amazed her: the more positive her attitude toward the friendship, the more David sought her company and the happier he seemed to be with her. As David began to seem more committed, Barbara, an excellent cook, began nonchalantly inviting both him and Brett to eat with her. In effect, she was using both the gourmet dinners and the positive attitude toward Brett as reinforcement for David's committed behavior. She found that David also seemed to respond to a cheerful attitude and gentle affection.

Over time, Barbara found herself profiting from our work in ways she had never dreamed of. She found that the more independence she achieved and the more fulfilled she became by her own separate interests, the stronger she became. Her mental picture of herself, who she was meant to be, became clearer and more cohesive. She also was more certain of what she wanted and didn't want, and about what she would and would not tolerate from David. Ultimately she felt more capable of taking care of herself should the relationship end. But that didn't happen. With less pressure on him, David became more comfortable with intimacy and with spending more time together. Eventually he was able to commit himself to engagement and finally marriage. His basic personality type didn't change; he remained fairly obsessive, while Barbara was not particularly so. Yet they were able to enrich both their lives by being together.

As I've often stated, most obsessives are graced with many wonderful qualities. Though they may at times be difficult, they have a lot to offer. Attention to the seven suggestions listed above should help the obsessive's friends, associates, and business partners establish relationships that, while not *perfect,* can nonetheless be deeply satisfying.

Epilogue

Habit is habit, and not to be flung out of the window, but coaxed downstairs a step at a time.

—MARK TWAIN

In summary, the obsessive personality style is a system of many normal traits, all aiming toward a common goal: safety and security via alertness, reason, and mastery. In rational and flexible doses, obsessive traits usually favor not only survival, but success and admiration as well.

The downside is that you can have too much of a good thing. You are bound for serious difficulties if your obsessive qualities serve not the simple goals of wise, competent, and enjoyable living, but an unrelenting need for fail-safe protection against the vulnerability inherent in being human. In this case, virtues become liabilities—exaggerated, rigid caricatures of themselves that greatly lessen your chances for happiness.

If you are a strongly obsessive person and are in pain, remember that although change is difficult, it's very possible. The single most important step is one you can take right now: acknowledge that the source of much of your unhappiness may not be your boss, the state of the economy, your spouse's shortcomings, or the untrustworthiness of others, but something within you! Acknowledge that the main obstacles to feeling fulfilled in your relationships, work, or leisure (if you have any) may be such things as your perfectionism, workaholism, rigidity, and other overdeveloped obsessive characteristics.

Open your mind to these possibilities, and change will have already begun! Just how far it will go is up to you. Motivation can take you a long way, and even small changes can pay enormous dividends.

In several chapters I offered a few specific suggestions of ways to help you move toward change. But please understand that this book is not a substitute for therapy with a competent professional. If you find that you aren't making progress despite motivation and reasonable effort, or if you find that as you work toward change you are developing symptoms such as severe anxiety, insomnia, gastrointestinal upsets, or depression, you probably will need some guidance and support. With or without professional assistance, your most important means to progress will be, quite simply, sustained hard work. But then that's your strong suit, isn't it?

SUGGESTED READINGS

The following list is a selection of interesting and pertinent writings on some of the topics presented in this book:

Obsessive Personality

American Psychiatric Association. *Diagnostic and Statistical Manual of Mental Disorders.* Third edition, revised (DSM-III-R), 354–56. Washington: APA, 1987.

Freud, Sigmund. "Character and Anal Erotism." In *The Standard Edition of the Complete Psychological Works of Sigmund Freud.* Edited by James Strachey. Vol. 9, 168–75. London: Hogarth Press, 1959.

Salzman, Leon. *Treatment of the Obsessive Personality.* New York: Jason Aronson, 1980.

Shapiro, David. "Obsessive-Compulsive Style." In *Neurotic Styles,* 23–53. New York: Basic Books, 1965.

Sullivan, Harry Stack. "Obsessionalism." In *The Collected Works of Harry Stack Sullivan.* Edited by Helen Swick Perry, Mary Ladd Gawel, and Martha Gibbon. Vol. II, 229–83. New York: Norton, 1956.

Obsessive-Compulsive Disorder (OCD)

American Psychiatric Association. *Diagnostic and Statistical Manual,* 245–47.

Freud, Sigmund. "The Rat Man." In *Standard Edition,* vol. 10, 153–326.

Jenike, Michael A., Lee Baer, and William E. Minichiello. *Obsessive Compulsive Disorders.* Littleton, Mass.: PSG Publishing, 1986.

Rapoport, Judith L. *The Boy Who Couldn't Stop Washing.* New York: Dutton, 1989.

Perfectionism, Workaholism, Need for Approval

Burns, David. *Feeling Good.* New York: Signet, 1980, 231–335.

INDEX